ANALYSIS OF TRANSFERENCE
VOLUME I
THEORY AND TECHNIQUE

ANALYSIS OF TRANSFERENCE
VOLUME I

THEORY AND TECHNIQUE

MERTON M. GILL

Psychological Issues
Monograph 53

INTERNATIONAL UNIVERSITIES PRESS, INC.
New York

Library of Congress Cataloging in Publication Data

Gill, Martin Max, 1914-
  Analysis of transference.

  (Psychological issues ; monograph 53-54)
  Vol. 2 by Merton M. Gill and Irwin Z. Hoffman also has title: Studies of nine audio-recorded psycho-analytic sessions.
  Bibliography: v. 1, p.   ; v. 2, p.
  Includes indexes.
  1. Transference (Psychology) 2. Transference (Psychology)—Case studies. I. Hoffman, Irwin Z. II. Title. III. Series. [DNLM: 1. Transference (Psychology) W1 PS572 monograph 53-54 / WM 62 G475a]
  RC489.T73G57   1982   616.89'17   81-23654
  ISBN 0-8236-0139-0 (v.1)   AACR2
  ISBN 0-8236-0140-4 (v. 2)

Manufactured in the United States of America

CONTENTS

ACKNOWLEDGMENTS

I express my indebtedness and thanks to Drs. Samuel D. Lipton, Irwin Hoffman, my collaborator on Volume II of this work, and Ilse Judas for their help in developing and clarifying the ideas in this monograph. This is not to imply that they agree with all I have written. My colleagues and students in a number of settings have also helped to shape these ideas in the many seminars and supervisory sessions in which they have been presented. I also wish to thank the successive chairmen under whom I have worked at the Abraham Lincoln School of Medicine — Drs. Melvin Sabshin, Hyman Muslin, and Lester Rudy — for their encouragement and for the freedom they have given me to work as I choose. Part of the work on this volume was supported by Research Scientist Award #19436 from the National Institute of Mental Health.

Grateful acknowledgment is also made to the following publishers for permission to include material from:

The Standard Edition of the Complete Psychological Works of Sigmund Freud, revised and edited by James Strachey, Sigmund Freud Copyrights Ltd., The Institute of Psycho-Analysis, and The Hogarth Press Ltd.

The Collected Papers of Sigmund Freud, Vol. 2, edited by Ernest Jones, M.D., authorized translation under the supervision of Joan Riviere, published by Basic Books, Inc., by arrangement with The Hogarth Press Ltd. and The Institute of Psycho-Analysis, London.

The Collected Papers of Sigmund Freud, Vol. 3, edited by Ernest Jones, M.D., authorized translation by Alix and James Strachey, published by Basic Books, Inc., by arrangement with The Hogarth Press Ltd. and The Institute of Psycho-Analysis, London.

The Collected Papers of Sigmund Freud, Vol. 5, edited by Ernest Jones,

M.D., and James Strachey, published by Basic Books, Inc., by arrangement with The Hogarth Press Ltd. and The Institute of Psycho-Analysis, London.

An Autobiographical Study, by Sigmund Freud, published by W. W. Norton and Company, Inc.

Beyond the Pleasure Principle, by Sigmund Freud, published by W. W. Norton and Company, Inc.

"Five Lectures on Psycho-Analysis," by Sigmund Freud, published by W. W. Norton and Company, Inc.

Group Psychology and the Analysis of the Ego, by Sigmund Freud, published by W. W. Norton and Company, Inc.

Introductory Lectures on Psycho-Analysis, by Sigmund Freud, published by Liveright Publishing Corp.

New Introductory Lectures on Psycho-Analysis, by Sigmund Freud, published by W. W. Norton and Company, Inc., and George Allen & Unwin Ltd.

The Question of Lay Analysis, by Sigmund Freud, published by W. W. Norton and Company, Inc.

An Outline of Psycho-Analysis, by Sigmund Freud, published by W. W. Norton and Company, Inc.

Studies on Hysteria, by Josef Breuer and Sigmund Freud, translated from the German and edited by James Strachey, in collaboration with Anna Freud, assisted by Alix Strachey and Alan Tyson, published in the United States by Basic Books, Inc., by arrangement with The Hogarth Press Ltd.

Problems of Psychoanalytic Technique, by Otto Fenichel, published by The Psychoanalytic Quarterly, Inc.

"The Widening Scope of Indications for Psychoanalysis: Discussion," by Anna Freud, published in *Journal of the American Psychoanalytic Association*, Vol. 2 (1954).

The Technique of Psychoanalysis, by Edward Glover, published by Balliere, Tindall & Cox.

"The Curative Factors in Psycho-Analysis," by Paula Heimann, published in *International Journal of Psycho-Analysis*, Vol. 43 (1962).

"The Curative Factors in Psycho-Analysis," by Pearl King, published in *International Journal of Psycho-Analysis*, Vol. 43 (1962).

"The Origins of Transference," by Melanie Klein, published in *International Journal of Psycho-Analysis*, Vol. 33 (1952).

"How the Mind of the Analyst Works," by Ishak Ramzy, published in *International Journal of Psycho-Analysis*, Vol. 55 (1974).

"Resistance to the Psychoanalytic Process," by Leo Stone, published in *Psychoanalysis and Contemporary Science: An Annual of Integrative and*

Interdisciplinary Studies, Vol. II, edited by Benjamin B. Rubinstein (copyright© 1973, Psychoanalysis and Contemporary Science, Inc.), excerpted with permission of The Free Press, a Division of Macmillan Publishing Co., Inc.

"The Psychoanalytic Situation and Transference," by Leo Stone, published in *Journal of the American Psychoanalytic Association*, Vol. 15 (1967).

"The Nature of the Therapeutic Action of Psycho-Analysis," by James Strachey, published in *International Journal of Psycho-Analysis*, Vol. 15 (1934).

INTRODUCTION

This monograph argues for a shift of emphasis in what I believe is prevailing opinion both in conceptualizing and analyzing the transference. My focus is on the centrality of analyzing the transference, not simply through classical genetic interpretation, but also, more importantly, through an understanding of the often largely implicit manifestations of the transference in the current analytic situation.

The context of the presentation is my opinion that psychoanalysis as it is generally practiced is not of good quality technically. In particular, I mean that the analysis of the transference, allegedly the heart of psychoanalytic technique, is not pursued consistently in practice.

The manner in which psychoanalysis is practiced makes it very difficult to substantiate such an opinion. I agree with Bird (1972), who writes that "nothing about analysis is less well known than how individual analysts actually use transference in their day-to-day work with patients" (p. 271). I base my opinion on hearing colleagues discuss cases, on supervision of psychoanalytic candidates, on the case material in our literature, and on the general tenor of the transcriptions of audio-recorded psychoanalytic sessions I have been able to gather. I must admit, of course, that in the latter case the sample is a selected one and quite possibly skewed. One might argue that those analysts who are willing to tape-record psychoanalytic sessions are in that very fact demonstrated to be practitioners who do not understand the centrality of transference. Otherwise they would recognize that the imposition of the recording situation on the analysis contaminates or distorts the transference to such a degree that a *bona fide* analysis is no longer possible. I disagree with

1

this argument, though I certainly recognize that those who are willing to audio-record analyses may very well differ from the usual run of psychoanalysts.

For the reader to understand my perspective, I also need to state my view of Freud's practice insofar as the analysis of the transference is concerned. I believe the principles of analytic technique were established very early, probably around 1898. Undoubtedly Freud's skill in dealing with the transference grew, as did his conviction in theory of its centrality (most notably expressed in the papers on technique of 1911–1915). Nevertheless, there was no major change in his theory of the role of the transference. Moreover, I believe that in practice he never gave the centrality to transference interpretation that it should have. Although his central theoretical focus is on the transference, in practice the analysis of the transference appears to have been ancillary to work with the neurosis in extra-transference terms. By "extra-transference" I intend the usual meaning of this term — outside the treatment situation. I am not thereby denying the role of transferences in the patient's life outside the treatment situation.

I must also describe a major trend in current analytic practice which contrasts with Freud's practice and is inferior to it. This trend has an important bearing on how the transference is analyzed. Freud was much freer in his interaction with the patient than analysts today are. The rationale for inhibiting the interaction with the patient is to make the transference stand out as sharply as possible from its interweaving with the actual situation, although the pursuit of this goal is often accompanied by the serious error of conceiving that nonresponsiveness does not contribute to the actual situation. Because the analytic situation is an interpersonal one, nonresponsiveness is part of the interaction too. Nonresponsiveness can become just as plausible a basis for an elaboration in the transference as any more obviously overt interaction can. While it is advisable to keep the interaction limited in scope and intensity, as judged by an outside observer, the transference is always and inevitably an interweaving of a contribution from the patient and the actual situation. Whatever the analyst does *not* do, as well as what he does do, will be the actuality around which the transference will weave.

Lipton (1977a) has suggested, in addition, that an overreaction to some analysts' tendency to use the relationship to manipulate the transference has led many analysts to restrict their interactions with the patient—even to the point of attempting to eliminate any personal relationship. He conceives of this as an overexpansion of what is encompassed by technique. At the same time he emphasizes that any interaction, even if not undertaken for technical reasons, may nevertheless have repercussions on the transference. Both the technical and nontechnical behaviors of the analyst are aspects of the actual situation and are therefore available to the patient as the rationale for and rationalization of the transference. My conclusion is that the analyst should have the freer kind of relationship with his patients that Freud had and that the transference can still be properly analyzed if the analyst takes account of the repercussions of his behavior, whether technical or nontechnical, on the transference.

My emphasis on the analysis of the transference may be misunderstood to mean that I advocate an aggressive, insistent analysis of the transference, without any regard for the repercussions such behavior by the analyst might have on the transference. The principle could of course be misapplied in this way. I am reminded of Fenichel's (1935) criticism of Wilhelm Reich that, correct though the principles he espoused were, he applied them in too militant a fashion. If the analysis of the transference is too aggressively applied, without recognition of how this influences the transference, that in itself is a violation of the principle I am arguing for. My position is always to take into account the manner in which the analyst's behavior becomes the point of departure for the patient's transference elaborations.

My focus on the analysis of the transference in the here-and-now should not be taken as a belittling of the importance of genetic transference interpretations. It is the priority of the former that I am advocating.

Although I have said that I believe the analysis of the transference is generally not well done at present, I also recognize that the technique of taking the actual situation into account in analyzing the transference is not something new but something that is surely done at least sporadically by all analysts and possibly systematically by some. I base that opinion in part on the fact that everything I have to say is already in our literature in one form or another. The demonstration of this is one reason for the extensiveness with which I quote from the literature.

If that is so, what contributions do I propose to make in this monograph? First, I believe I have achieved a systematic organization and an emphasis which are in fact new. My hope is that the reader may come to believe something akin to what Fenichel said of Reich: "In so far as these principles are merely elaborations of Freud's views, they are 'nothing new'; in so far as they are *consistent elaborations* of it, they *are* something new" (1935, p. 453). I hope therefore to have some impact on those whose failure to make transference interpretations appropriately has a significant intellectual base and not primarily an emotional one.

Second, the literature includes serious differences of opinion on the issues I shall consider. I hope that my presentation will move the reader toward my stand on these issues.

Third, I concede that reading about technique runs a poor third as a way of learning technique, compared with one's own analysis and one's experience in conducting analyses, first under supervision and then alone. Nevertheless, the value of a coherent systematic intellectual framework is far from negligible.

Furthermore, while Volume I of this monograph focuses on theory and technique, Volume II, written in collaboration with Irwin Z. Hoffman, offers a detailed discussion of the transcripts of audio-recorded sessions. These transcripts have been selected from a number of analyses and psychotherapies to illustrate typical issues in the analysis of the transference. Dr. Hoffman and I are of the opinion that only with the presentation of this detailed material will it become clear what we intend by giving the analysis of the transference priority and primacy in the analytic process. It is easy to give lip service to the principle and not really carry it through. We shall, for instance, include examples of overzealous transference interpretation which fails to recognize the repercussions on the transference of this overzealousness. Therapists who become persuaded of the importance of interpreting the transference are particularly prone to this error in their early enthusiasm.

Most of the case material in our literature is in the summary form of vignettes. Glover (1955) indicates that adequate case illustration requires an inordinate amount of space. According to him:

> Many analysts attempt to overcome this difficulty by subjecting their material to processes of condensation, selection and secondary elaboration, finally presenting the readers with a compact, well-rounded and apparently convincing digest. Needless to say, from the scientific point of view this is a thoroughly unsatisfactory procedure which opens the door to every variety of tendentiousness and has in fact greatly reduced the credit and the credibility of analytic interpretations [pp. vii–viii].

Glover concludes that the original data of analytic sessions cannot be presented and restricts himself to "thumbnail sketches." In his view, audio-recording is not permissible, in part because it would interfere with the spontaneity of the "countertransference." Moreover, he contends that audio-recording fails to communicate "much of what is important in the psycho-analytic process." But what Glover does not consider is the different impact of a summary of extensive material and a verbatim presentation of a limited segment. To my mind, technique must be demonstrated and learned from verbatim transcribed (or listened to) sessions, as well as from summaries either of single sessions or of numbers of sessions. The examination of the microscopic details of the process reveals much that summaries omit.

A third kind of presentation entails systematic research on the psychoanalytic situation. The principles of the analysis of the transference discussed in Volume I have led to the development of a scheme for coding transcribed psychoanalytic and psychotherapeutic sessions according to how the transference is handled (including its mishandling or its disregard). This scheme, arrived at with the collaboration of Dr. Hoffman, provides a basis for both systematic and meaningful research (see Gill and Hoffman, 1982).

Indeed, it is my opinion that the absence of systematic research is one important reason that even though the principles I espouse can be extracted from our literature, they are often not integral to practice. It is only with such research that empirical findings are nailed down and theory becomes common and secure knowledge, divorced from the reputation and prestige of its originator. One may liken this situation to how an identification, which is at first an introject, must become divested of the earmarks of its origin if it is to become genuinely integrated into the ego. I am reminded of a statement Freud quoted approvingly from Goethe's Faust: "What thou hast inherited from thy fathers, acquire it to make it thine" (Freud, 1940, p. 207).

With this as my perspective, I shall pursue the following course. First I shall try to clarify three issues that are often confused: (1) the difference between the facilitating transference, which Freud called the unobjectionable positive transference, and the obstructing transference, which he called the transference resistance; (2) the distinction between interpreting resistance to the awareness of transference and resistance to the resolution of transference; and (3) the discriminations between the overlapping terms employed for various relationships between transference and resistance. My proposal here is that because of a confusion of resistance with defense, it is not recognized that all resistance manifests itself in the transference.

In arguing for the centrality of the transference in analytic work, I begin by citing Freud's two models — the one in which the transference is ancillary and the other in which it becomes the heart of the analytic work. As will be shown, Freud's position was that the repetition of the past should be encouraged as much as possible in the transference within the analytic situation because it is best dealt with there, but he was not explicit about how this should be promoted. Here it is important to consider not only how the analytic setup itself promotes this repetition, but also how the analyst must look for allusions to the transference in associations that are not manifestly about the transference. I shall then discuss the ubiquity of transference, in connection with which I shall examine the distinction between transferences and the transference neurosis proper. I shall also deal with the early interpretation of transference.

Turning to how the interpretation of resistance to awareness of the transference should take the actual analytic situation into account, I shall first point out how the interpersonal nature of the analytic situation means that all transference must be related to the actual situation. An articulation of the interpreting of both resistance to the awareness of the transference and resistance to its resolution follows. Work on the latter entails both comparing the patient's attitudes with other possible ways of experiencing the actual situation, with which they are intertwined, and examining the new experience itself, as it is engendered in the analysis of the interaction between patient and analyst. Here I do not deny the importance of genetic transference interpretations and working through. My position is simply that transference interpretations in the here-and-now are often wrongly slighted in favor of genetic transference interpretations and that priority in working through must go to the transference in the present.

My next concern is with the Kleinians' position on transference interpretation. Their stance is relevant here because they stress the analysis of the transference more than other analysts do. But their underemphasis on the actual analytic situation leads them to both too "deep" interpretations and too exclusive a focus on the genetics of the transference (which I think may have caused other analysts to overreact and downplay the transference).

In a last chapter I reexamine Freud's approach to the transference. I begin with a historical review, more understandable in the light of my presentation than it would have been had I started with it. I present evidence that Freud did indeed slight the analysis of the transference in practice. I believe that discoverer of the transference though he was, his legacy must now be superseded if the analysis of the transference is to have its due.

I have written this monograph in terms of the analysis of the transference in psychoanalysis. The question arises of the applicability of the principles I describe to patients who are seen less often, for a more limited duration, or to those who are sicker than those ordinarily considered analyzable. I believe the same principles can and should be used in these other circumstances. I have discussed this issue elsewhere (Gill, 1979, 1982) and shall not take it up here. It would be an error to call such work "psychotherapy" because that term implies that psychoanalytic techniques are either not used or are used in modified form. I believe that all psychological therapy other than avowedly "supportive" therapy should attempt to analyze the transference in the way I describe here.

1

WHAT IS MEANT BY
INTERPRETATION OF TRANSFERENCE?

The concept of transference is itself somewhat unclear. To begin with, although Freud distinguished between facilitating and obstructing transferences, many writers recognize only obstructing transference. Others are aware of the distinction but consider the concept of facilitating transference unfortunate and misleading. Beyond this confusion, two ideas are condensed in the phrase "the interpretation of transference," namely, interpretation of resistance to the *awareness* of transference and interpretation of resistance to the *resolution* of transference. The former is the one most often slighted in practice and least explicitly focused on in our literature. For this reason, I shall give several examples of interpretation of resistance to the awareness of transference.

FACILITATING AND OBSTRUCTING TRANSFERENCES

Freud discusses and classifies transference from the vantage point of the analyst as observer. From that viewpoint he notes that transferences can be either appropriate or inappropriate to the actual analytic situation. He calls the first, the unobjectionable positive transference, and the second, transference resistance.

The failure clearly to understand that for Freud transference means a person's way of relating leads to the incorrect, restrictive conceptualization of transference in terms of the repressed basis of that way of relating. Freud (1912a) explicitly states that the "stereotype plate" of the person's way of relating includes an

9

aspect which has "passed through the full process of psychical development," is "directed towards reality," and is available to the "conscious personality" (p. 100). This aspect forms the unobjectionable positive transference. It is important to clarify that Freud is referring not to the feelings in the present but to the basis of those feelings in the past. However conscious, unobjectionable, and directed toward reality these feelings may be, this aspect of the transference is still heavily dependent on past experience.

In the papers on technique Freud distinguishes positive and negative transferences and further subdivides positive transferences into friendly or affectionate feelings and their unconscious erotic sources. According to Freud, we do not fully "remove" the transference by bringing it into the light of consciousness. What we detach from the perception of the analyst are the negative and erotic components of the patient's transference. The "other component, which is admissible to consciousness and unobjectionable, persists and is the vehicle of success in psycho-analysis exactly as it is in other methods of treatment" (1912a, p. 105).

Thus Freud includes in the transference not only the repetition of repressed elements in the person's "stereotype plate" which are inappropriate to the present, but also its conscious and appropriate elements. This point is clearly seen in his remark: "The peculiarities of the transference to the doctor . . . are made intelligible if we bear in mind that this transference has precisely been set up not only by the *conscious* anticipatory ideas but also by those that have been held back or are unconscious" (1912a, p. 100).

Freud's inclusion of the conscious, appropriate elements of the person's way of relating in his concept of transference has often been criticized. Loewenstein (1969), for example, considers that Freud uses the word "transference" inappropriately for what Loewenstein refers to as deriving from "an alliance between the analyst and the healthy part of the patient's ego" (p. 586). In Loewenstein's opinion, what Freud calls the "positive transference," which embraces the patient's feelings of confidence and hope in the analyst, needs to be distinguished from the transference proper. Citing Sterba (1934), Zetzel (1958), and Greenson (1965), Loewenstein indicates that the patient's willingness to cooperate in the analysis "is not transference in the strict sense of the term" (p. 586). Much earlier, Hendrick (1939) similarly stipulated: "The practice of using 'transference' as though synonymous with 'rapport' or 'friendly feelings' is quite unjustified and confusing" (pp. 194n–195n). Silverberg (1948) also expresses this view.

Rather than finding Freud's use of "transference" for both the conscious and repressed bases of the patient's way of relating "unjustified and confusing," I believe it does grave violence to Freud's concept of transference and its major role in the analytic process to exclude its conscious, "unobjectionable" roots. Freud in fact readily admits the use of suggestion (or transference) as a tool of psychoanalysis (1912a, p. 106), but he notes a difference in this use from other therapeutic techniques: "It is used [in analysis] to induce the patient to perform a piece of psychical work — the overcoming of his transference-resistances — which involves a permanent alteration in his mental economy. . . . In this way the transference is changed from the strongest weapon of the resistance into the best instrument of the analytic treatment" (1925, p. 43). Here Freud not only distinguishes between transference and transference resistance, but also describes the use of the transference itself to assist in overcoming the transference resistance.

"When are we to begin making our communications to the patient?" he asks (1913, p. 139). And he answers: "Not until an effective transference has been established with the patient, a proper *rapport* with him." The formation of this attachment to the analyst's person is the first goal, and all that the patient needs to do this is time. Yet, in saying this, Freud is not ruling out any activity by the analyst. "If one exhibits a serious interest in [the patient], carefully clears away the resistances that crop up at the beginning and avoids making certain mistakes, he will of himself form such an attachment and link the doctor up with one of the imagos of the people by whom he was accustomed to be treated with affection" (pp. 139–140). Moreover, the analyst may lose "this first success" by assuming some judgmental stance or taking the side of "some contending party" (p. 140).

The role of the analyst's behavior in the analytic situation is a topic I shall later deal with in detail. Here I wish only to point out that Freud deemphasizes the role of the analyst's behavior in determining the character of the transference. He states, for example:

> In every analytic treatment there arises, without the physician's agency, an intense emotional relationship between the patient and the analyst which is not to be accounted for by the actual situation.... This *transference*—to give it its short name—soon replaces in the patient's mind the desire to be cured.... We can easily recognize it as the same dynamic factor which the hypnotists have named 'suggestibility', which is the agent of hypnotic *rapport* [1925, p. 42].

By suggestibility Freud means "a conviction which is not based upon perception and reasoning but upon an erotic tie" (1921, p. 128). He is talking about "influenceability." As Loewald (1960) says: "Transference in this sense is virtually synonymous with object-cathexis" (p. 27). The very term "transference neurosis" is used to describe a neurosis in which the patient is influenceable *because* he has the capacity for relating positively. In other words, Freud names the transference neurosis with reference to the conscious, unobjectionable positive transference, not the repressed, inappropriate transference. The unobjectionable positive transference is clearly a transference for Freud in that it is significantly determined by the past. In emphasizing this, Freud even understates the role of the analyst's behavior in the present in determining the character of the transference.

That the transference is often defined as "distorting" a realistic relationship shows a lack of recognition that Freud's inclusion of the conscious, unobjectionable positive transference in his concept of transference is not an unfortunate lapse but an integral aspect of the concept. Both Anna Freud and Greenson make this mistake. Anna Freud defines transference (and countertransference) in terms of "the distortion of a realistic patient-analyst relationship by additions from past unconscious and repressed object relations" (1968, pp. 95–96). Greenson explains: *"Transference is the experiencing of feeling, drives, attitudes, fantasies, and defenses toward a person in the present which do not befit that person but are a repetition of reactions originating in regard to significant persons of early childhood, unconsciously displaced onto figures in the present"* (1967, p. 171).

Fenichel (1938–1939) makes the same error. He describes a "rational transference," which is the same as Freud's unobjectionable positive transference. But he misunderstands Freud's concept in assuming that Freud's unobjectionable positive transference must be irrational just because it has important determinants in the past. In line with this, Fenichel indicates that his own term "rational transference" is in itself a contradiction since, in his opinion, the notion of transference inevitably entails the unrealistic reading of the past into the present situation. Thus, Fenichel concludes that while the positive transference may at times "be very welcome during long periods of an analysis as a motive for overcoming resistances . . . *insofar as it is transference*, the impulses belong to infantile objects, and therefore a time must come when these same transference impulses become resistances, and their true relationship must be demonstrated to the patient" (pp. 27–28). In contrast, as we have already seen, Freud (1925) is explicit that the unobjectionable positive transference does not require analysis.

Stone (1961) also defines a "mature transference," comparable to Freud's unobjectionable positive transference. But, unlike Fenichel, he does not insist that it must ultimately be analyzed. He believes the mature transference must be gratified to some degree for an analysis to proceed satisfactorily. According to Stone, the analyst's understanding and "the germane emotional attitude constitute central and essential 'gratifications' for the patient's 'mature transference' strivings, enabling his toleration, even positive utilization of the principle of abstinence, in relation to primitive transference demands" (p. 80). Stone sees the mature transference as allowing for "insight as an autonomous ego function, as opposed to its primitive transference or symptomatic functions, in the sense described by Ernst Kris [1956b]" (p. 93). Note that he does not say that the mature transference *is* the autonomous function but that it is the *basis* for it.

By "mature transference" Stone decidedly means a transference in the sense of an attitude significantly determined by the *past*. He clearly defines the mature transference as "a nonrational urge, not directly dependent on the perception of immediate clinical purposes, a true 'transference' in the sense that it is displaced (in currently relevant form) from the parent of early childhood to the analyst" (1967, p. 24).

Stone's view that the mature transference must be gratified to some degree surely says no more than Freud implied in the personal relations he had with his patients, in the context of which he made his technical interventions. Neither Stone nor Freud means this gratification of the mature transference to be deliberately engaged in as a technical device.

The distinction between the unobjectionable positive transference and other transferences is in fact a distinction between transference that facilitates the analytic process and transference that resists the process. However, because Freud intimates so often that the positive transference is used to overcome the resistance, it is easy to be misled and to fail to realize that the positive transference is only the prerequisite for the analytic work. As we already noted, Freud states that the transference is used to "induce the patient to perform a piece of psychical work" (1925, p. 42) — to *induce* to perform, not to perform. The distinction is not accidental. It also appears in the paper on "The Dynamics of Transference" (1912a): "We take care of the patient's final independence by employing suggestion in order to get him to accomplish a piece of psychical work which has as its necessary result a permanent improvement in his psychical situation" (p. 106). And in the *Introductory Lectures* Freud points out: "This work of overcoming resistances is the essential function of analytic treatment; the patient has to accomplish it and the doctor makes this possible for him with the help of suggestion operating in an *educative* sense" (1916–1917, p. 451).

Another passage, from Freud's essay "On Beginning the Treatment" (1913), also clearly contrasts transference as facilitator to transference as resistance. In this case, the former is called transference and the latter transference resistance. It is the (positive) transference that makes the patient able to attend to the analyst's communications: "The patient, however, only makes use of the instruction in so far as he is induced to do so by the transference; and it is for this reason that our first communication should be withheld until a strong transference has been established. And this, we may add, holds good of every subsequent communication. In each case we must wait until the disturbance of the transference by the successive emergence of transference-resistances has been removed" (p. 144).

Fenichel (1935) makes the same distinction I have made between facilitating transference and obstructing transference,
even to the point of calling the former "facilitating." He comments: "In analytic therapy. . . transference (except for its positive, affectionate form, which to begin with facilitates the overcoming of other resistances) becomes fundamentally a resistance,
and must be recognized and worked through as such" (p. 464).
Yet Fenichel implies that the facilitating aspect applies only at
the beginning, as an initial motivation.

The term "unobjectionable positive transference" per se plays
little role in the literature after Freud, probably because Freud
employs it only in passing. I have chosen to refer to it as facilitating transference since that captures the way Freud uses it in
contrast to transference resistance. It would be misleading to
use it to mean simply the realistic attitude to the analyst, because, although the positive transference is consonant with the
reality, it is significantly dependent on the past and it is this latter aspect that Freud emphasizes.

RESISTANCE TO THE AWARENESS OF TRANSFERENCE AND RESISTANCE TO THE RESOLUTION OF TRANSFERENCE

One can speak alternatively of the "analysis of the transference" or the "interpretation of the transference." Both of these
phrases imply making explicit something that is implicit because of resistance. They are both shorthand for analysis of
transference resistance, since the facilitating transference is conscious, unobjectionable, and not resisted. But these equivalent
phrases also condense two meanings which must be separated
for clarity. One is the interpretation that a content which is
manifestly about something other than the transference includes
a hidden allusion to transference. The other is the interpretation
that a content which is manifestly about the relationship is indeed transference in the sense of having important determinants outside as well as within the current analytic situation, or,
in Freud's words, elements "not to be accounted for by the actual situation" (1925, p. 42).

On a descriptive level the distinction can be seen as a difference between interpreting indirect or implicit references to the relationship in contrast to direct or explicit references to the relationship. Direct references to the analyst, however, may also conceal indirect allusions to the transference as, for example, in positive expressions that are a denial of negative transference and vice versa. Furthermore, direct references to the analyst are not necessarily expressions of transference resistance, since they may be realistically appropriate to the actual situation, as well as having the roots in the past that are ubiquitous to all behavior. On the other hand, indirect references to the analyst are undoubtedly transference resistance if the indirectness stems from an inability to speak directly about a particular idea relating to the analyst.

Both kinds of interpretation of the transference are of course exemplified in Freud's writings and are in the repertoire of every analyst, but they are not distinguished sharply enough. When Freud discusses the erotic transference of a woman who is satisfied only with "the logic of soup, with dumplings for arguments" (1915, p. 167), he is clearly talking about directly expressed attitudes to the analyst which are a displacement from elsewhere. But when he explains in his postscript to the Dora case (1905) that one has to deduce the transference from tiny clues and that he missed seeing in Dora's talk about Herr K. the displaced feelings about himself which ultimately led to her flight from the treatment, he is speaking of an indirect reference to the transference. It is this kind of indirect allusion to the analyst which Freud failed to interpret systematically in the Dora case, as Muslin and I (1978) have emphasized.

Although our literature often refers to this distinction, it is not often sharply focused on nor are there clearly agreed-upon terms for the two kinds of transference interpretation. Wisdom (1956), for instance, points out three different situations to which the designation "interpretation of the transference" has been applied. The first type involves the clarification of a particular relationship between the patient and the analyst, such as the patient's fear that the analyst will retaliate in anger. Wisdom refers to this as "an analytic-situation" or "patient-analyst interpretation." The second kind of interpretation links several associations to point to a similar relationship obtaining between the patient and the various people in his present life situation. This is what Wisdom calls "an environment-interpretation." Finally, there is the interpretation that underlines the similarity to a relationship from the patient's childhood past, or what Wisdom terms the "childhood interpretation." As Wisdom indicates, the classical definition of "transference interpretation" refers to the analyst's "pointing out the third and first together or rather the carryover of the relationship in the third to the first." He also notes that many analysts use this term "for the carryover from the second to the first (which is also known as a 'here-and-now' interpretation), although they would generally have the childhood situation in mind" (pp. 148–149).

Of the three types described by Wisdom, the first corresponds to what I have distinguished as the interpretation of an allusion to the transference, while the second and third correspond to the interpretation that an attitude toward the analyst is indeed transference—by pointing out either that the patient's attitude in the treatment is the same as his attitude toward "all the people in his environment" or that it is the same as an attitude from his childhood. Wisdom refers to this as a parallel (in the second type) between the outside present and the analytic relationship and a "carryover" (in the third type) from the outside past to the analytic relationship.

The names he proposes, however, are not commonly accepted in our literature. One does sometimes see a reference to an interpretation of the here-and-now relationship in the treatment, but it is more likely to mean what I have called an interpretation of an allusion to the transference than what Wisdom calls a parallel between the outside present and the treatment relationship. Wisdom's third type is often called a genetic transference interpretation.

Freud himself often uses the term "transference" to refer to the carryover from the past to the present. Nevertheless, he does use it with respect to the current analytic situation alone. He explains that once "the treatment has obtained mastery over the patient, what happens is that the whole of his illness's new production is concentrated upon a single point—his relation to the doctor.... When the transference has risen to this significance, work upon the patient's memories retreats far into the background" (1916–1917, p. 444).

Stone (1967) believes that the term "transference interpretation," at least in current usage, "refers not so much to the genetic interpretation of the current transference attitude, as it means a concise direct statement to the patient of an attitude towards the analyst which is at the moment active, but unconscious or, possibly more often, preconscious" (p. 48). Stone's distinctions here correspond to Wisdom's third and first kinds. Wisdom's second—the interpretation of a parallel between an attitude in the analytic situation and the contemporary external situation—is not often specified. I have thus omitted it from my classification of types of transference interpretations.

Analytic work is such that a terminological distinction between the two kinds of transference interpretation is desirable. Both kinds are necessary, and they constitute a sequence. There is often a great deal of work in making the patient aware of his attitudes in the relationship before one has the data in hand which enable one to interpret that these attitudes are indeed transference. Moreover, the patient must become aware of a transference before work toward its resolution can begin.

In line with this, I believe that the two major kinds of transference interpretation can be best characterized as dealing with two different manifestations of resistance. The interpretation of an allusion to the transference is an interpretation of resistance to the awareness of transference, while the interpretation that the attitude is indeed transference is an interpretation of resistance to the resolution of transference, or, as Stone (1973) puts it, "the reduction" of transference.

Here I must introduce yet another distinction. I shall later emphasize that some interpretations of resistance to the resolution of transference are made solely *within* the data of the current analytic situation, by showing that the patient's attitude is not unequivocally determined by the features of the actual analytic situation on which the patient partly bases it. There are then two ways of interpreting resistance to the resolution of transference—the one just described and the one that draws a parallel between the patient's attitude and an early "genetic" attitude or experience.

The distinctions I shall use in this monograph are outlined below. Under *transference interpretations* we find:

1. Interpretations of resistance to the awareness of transference. For example: "The episode you told me about your wife is an allusion to something similar which you feel is going on between us but which you are reluctant to mention."

2. Interpretations of resistance to the resolution of transference.

(a) Interpretations that work with the transference in the here-and-now, by pointing out, for instance, that a particular attitude is not so clearly determined by aspects of the actual analytic situation as the patient contends. For example: "You believe that I am uneasy about the homosexual wish toward me which you expressed yesterday, and you consider that I am revealing that by the questions I asked about your sexual relationship with your wife. Yet you recognize that you told me about this episode with her with omissions that seem designed to get me to ask questions about it."

(b) "Genetic transference interpretations," or interpretations of a similarity between the transference attitude and the past. For example: "Your belief that I am always critical of you is very similar to what you believed your father's attitude to be." (This is the same definition of "genetic transference interpretation" that both Wisdom [1956] and Stone [1967] use.)

These three kinds of interpretations all involve transference, whether as such or in connection with something else. There are also two types of *extra-transference interpretations*, which make no reference to the transference (confining the designation "transference" to the relation between patient and analyst):

1. "Contemporary interpretations," or interpretations directed solely at a contemporary extra-transference situation. For example: "You must have felt jealous when your wife told you that, though you were apparently unaware of it."

2. "Genetic interpretations," or interpretations referring solely to an early extra-transference situation. For example: "You must have felt that your mother didn't love you anymore because of the new baby." (This is the kind of interpretation Freud

calls a "reconstruction," though he also specifies that the term denotes a fairly elaborate plot rather than a relatively isolated point.)

Illustrations

To make sure that my distinctions are quite clear I shall offer several illustrations of interpretation of resistance to the awareness of transference at this point. I have chosen to emphasize the kind of transference interpretation that clarifies a possible allusion to the transference rather than the "genetic" kind, which explicates the transference by revealing its roots in the past. The first two examples are taken from audio-recorded sessions of patients seen once a week.

In the first instance, the patient, herself a psychotherapist, describes her own vigorous interpretations, which were designed to arouse a patient who had withdrawn into lethargy. She then shifts to discussing her inability to reach orgasm in intercourse but does so in a halting, elliptical manner. The therapist interprets that she wants him to make vigorous interpretations to her as she had done with her patient. This interpretation of resistance to the awareness of transference paves the way to understanding how she equates interpretations with sexual activity.

In the second case, the patient missed a session. Although he telephoned beforehand to set up a mutually suitable time, he forgot this appointment. At his next regular hour, he describes an interaction with his wife in which he felt she had made an unreasonable request of him and had done so in a demanding manner. The therapist interprets that the patient feels that the therapist forced him to accept an inconvenient time. The patient rejects the interpretation, saying that it was he who asked for the substitute time. The therapist then interprets that the patient believes the therapist felt he had been forced to grant the patient's request. In the first interpretation the therapist is represented as playing the wife's role while the patient's role is unchanged. In the second interpretation the patient is represented as the wife and the therapist as the patient. As I shall discuss again later, the first interpretation is one of displacement in the transference while the second is one of identification in the transference (see Lipton, 1977b). In the first interpretation the patient remains himself both outside and inside the transference. In the second interpretation the associations about the interaction with the wife are interpreted as alluding in the transference to the patient in the role of the wife with the therapist in the role of the patient. In other words, in the story outside the transference the patient is identified with what he believes the therapist is feeling inside the transference. Neither interpretation is meant to question the validity of the patient's experience outside the transference. All that is implied is that the associations include an allusion to the transference.

A third example comes from a recent presentation by Ishak Ramzy (1974), which includes a portion of a verbatim transcript of an analytic session. While I shall be critical of Ramzy, I do not regard his interpretations as at all uncommon in practice and I emphasize that Ramzy has laid himself open to criticism only because he has had the courage to present verbatim material.

As soon as the patient enters, Ramzy explains, he lies down and begins talking:

Well, before I came up here I went back home since I forgot to leave a cheque with my cleaning lady. Well, she wasn't around and when I was driving up here I was kind of worried. She is sort of an old lady, maybe in her late 50s or early 60s. Maybe she's sick or some such. So I was telling myself while I was driving up here I better go and call some friend of mine and see what happened to her. And immediately it also struck me that: 'Well, what if she is really sick and can't work?' That would be kind of horrible. In Kansas a cleaning lady is not so easy to find, especially the one that you don't have to tell her what to do and she will just automatically do. Well, then I began to think. 'What did I do before I found her?' I remember before I found her there was another one I had, then she moved out to California. Well then, what happened before the one I had? Well, well, thinking of it, that was very funny because now I remember before I had all these cleaning ladies and when I first came to Kansas; every couple of months or so I would get really depressed because wherever I lived it is going to be so dirty and so messy and sometime I have to really get enough energy to really do a thorough cleaning for a whole week practically. So I haven't faced this for quite some years and I didn't remember how it used to be. It was pretty horrible. In any event, I hope nothing happened or else it will be a big hunting job [p. 546].

Ramzy indicates that the patient then shifts to another subject and goes on in detail about his students' difficulties in "studying for his course, their abilities and their goals, graduate and undergraduate levels and so on." After some 15 minutes of this, the analyst intervenes:

Your earlier thoughts about the cleaning lady which occurred to you on the way here and your worry over losing her make me think that they may be connected with my upcoming absence for the next two weeks, starting next Monday [p. 546].

There now follows a struggle between the patient and the analyst in which the analyst attempts to justify his interpretation in the teeth of the patient's resistance. The analyst's interpretation is a very good example of a transference interpretation based on associations which are not explicitly about the transference. But I choose this illustration also to call attention to Ramzy's statement that the patient changed the subject and began to talk about his students' difficulties. That Ramzy lets this talk go on for 15 minutes before bringing the patient back to the thoughts about the cleaning lady and makes no suggestion about the possible implications for the transference of the patient's remarks about his students suggests that he may not have realized that the apparently changed subject also had implications for the transference. It might well be that had he dealt with the possible transference implications of this talk about students and integrated these conclusions with those about the cleaning lady, he would have been able to make his interpretation more meaningful to the patient. At least he might have been able to make a transference interpretation closer to the patient's awareness than the one about the cleaning lady. Because he does not give the verbatim material of the associations about the students, it is impossible for me to suggest what implications they might have had for the transference, but it is not unlikely that the difficulties his students were encountering allude either to his difficulties with the analyst or to the analyst's with him.

The excerpt is an example of what I believe is a common practice. Though analysts undoubtedly frequently make interpretations of resistance to the awareness of transference on the basis of associations not explicitly about the transference, they are likely to make such interpretations only sporadically, either because they are not aware of the widespread applicability of the principle or because they do not consider it good technique to give priority to the interpretation of the transference wherever possible.

The examination of verbatim material invariably allows a vigilant observer to recognize many instances of possible interpretations of resistance to the awareness of transference which were overlooked. Hindsight, and the leisure to examine the material repeatedly, provides many insights the analyst conducting the session will have missed.

Incidentally, if one is dealing with the verbatim transcript of an isolated session, one may well miss transference interpretations which the analyst with a full knowledge of the sessions is in a position to make. In Ramzy's case, for instance, how would we know that the analyst was about to be absent for two weeks if he had not said so in an interpretation?

My fourth example is from an audio-recorded analytic session. It illustrates a plausible interpretation of resistance to the awareness of transference which might have been made but was not.

This segment presents what may be a very common sequence for a patient's associations. At the beginning of the hour, the patient makes a few scattered, brief remarks about the analytic relationship, followed by material which in manifest content is not about the relationship. The alert analyst will see in the nontransference associations a continuation of the theme broached in the initial explicit allusions to the relationship and be able thereby to make an interpretation of an allusion to the transference.

In this particular session the patient begins by describing her eagerness to come to the hour to discuss something and her reluctance to do so now that the hour has begun. This is followed by her describing a sexual episode with her husband in which she was eager to begin but then found herself reluctant to continue. Extracting the material in this bald way from the mass of associations in which it is embedded makes it obvious that there is some relationship between the explicit relationship material and the subsequent associations about the sexual episode with her husband. A possible interpretation would be that the patient-analyst relationship is viewed as a sexual encounter. In the actual session the sequence is not as apparent as it is in this description. In order to make the illustration as clarifying as possible, the verbatim transcript of the first few minutes is presented here.

[Silence] Well, thinking of several things all quickly together and, umm, the first thing was just that when I, umm, rearranged the pillow I was thinking of the time before when I had had my hair like this a lot and [clears throat] at one point I had the pillow so far up it would probably fall off and I noticed that you hit it today [that is, as the analyst sat down]. So I was thinking, "Well, it must be practically ready to fall off." And, umm, well, I, I didn't know; first I guess I was just wondering, "Is my attitude the same as it had been before when I was doing that?" But then immediately I thought of my baby sitter and, umm, I don't know whether it all kind of happened that I would think of her because she came and met me at the park today and I felt I wanted to be on time today. And, umm, so I left a lot earlier. Well, and I needed to leave earlier from the park than I would at home because it's further, but I even left earlier than I thought I might have from the park, according to what time I thought I would think I would have to go. And, umm, but then I started thinking about sort of a combination of how she's always been kind of strange when I met; she's come to meet me at the park and take care of my baby and, umm, I don't know, just very cold and sort of unfriendly. And she was today. But then I was thinking, "But otherwise she's been a lot nicer and happier," so—I think I've said this before—I've begun to realize how unhappy she's been in the spring. And then I was thinking, well, I wonder how final it is that she's coming back because she has been given a definite assignment for the summer at the nursing home and it's not a permanent job, ah, which would mean, unless something happens to change it, that she'll come back with us. And, I don't know, I was just thinking of the fact that after thinking of trying to move closer to you then I think of the baby sitter. And it seems like before I've thought of her, umm, and I've never been sure if I'm thinking of her because [clears throat], I don't know, it's just something to think of instead of the thought that I want to get away from, or if it's that she really fits in somehow, because of being a woman and, and my having to deal with her. And then her name, too—I know I wondered about that before. And another thing that's on my mind is, which has been, umm, I don't know, I think which—well, again, I have this feeling, I've had it sometimes before, of being eager to get here and talk about something that was a continuation from the day before but then once I get here I feel more reluctant. And it's, I, I don't know, I feel as if it's true now, too, that I think I was having the feeling, which I suddenly don't have, of, umm, wanting to talk about the fact that last night, after our guests went—they left at a pretty good time so we didn't get to bed very late, and then my husband wanted to make love. And it was, at first, sort of a similar situation to the night before that I described yesterday. But, umm, I was more open in admitting I knew what he was doing and maybe he was more positive that he wanted to make love, I'm not sure which. But anyway, I certainly was more open in recognizing what he was trying to say to me.

The material continues with a description of her reaching orgasm through cunnilingus and then his having an orgasm in her vagina, after which she began to feel nauseated. She now suggests that was probably because she had had an orgasm and continues:

> I just had an overwhelming feeling of what I talked about yesterday, of, umm, finding it unbearable to have him start to arouse me or to feel that I was being aroused and, umm, wanting to stop it, and yet, on the other hand, really wanting not to stop it.

The additional details in the verbatim content are very readily integrated into an interpretation that the description of the sexual episode with her husband is an implicit continuation of the earlier, explicit transference material. The business about the pillow's being pushed back, so that the analyst's knee hit it when he sat down, she interprets herself as possibly meaning that she was trying to move closer to him (which is also consistent with the idea that the wish to come early has a sexual implication). The meeting with the baby sitter, who seemed cold and unfriendly, could similarly be understood as implying that either she or the analyst is being cold and unfriendly, as well as suggesting a desire for sexual contact and then inhibition of the desire.

In this session the analyst fails to make a transference interpretation. Subsequent material in the session, which I shall not give here, continues to deal with situations in which the patient simultaneously felt sexual desire and an inhibition of that desire. My argument here is for the desirability of an intepretation that would have suggested an allusion to the early explicit references to the analytic situation in the material about herself and her husband.[1]

Illustrations of this sort could be endlessly multiplied. Here is one culled from Glover's (1955) book on technique. The patient had had some previous analysis. Glover describes how the session begins with this woman's comparing two servants. One of them is "cheerful and impertinent, but sometimes helpful," while the other is "phlegmatic, heavy, unenterprising, but quite respectful" (p. 116). Glover understands this as follows:

> ...the impertinent maid is the earlier analyst, the lumpish one myself. She resented the explanations given by the former, reading them as sexual advances; and yet, whilst fearing them, she liked them. Hence, she is reproaching me for my impotence or incapacity. The theme being about servants, there is probably some play on the word "service" as well as a veiled depreciating tendency [pp. 116–117].

Earlier in his book, Glover states this principle of interpretation more generally:

> When after stumbling utterances on, let us say, the subject of masturbation, the patient dwells on the obnoxious characteristics of authoritative figures in his environment, their tendency to unwarranted interference or unfair criticism, we are able to relate these reactions to the immediate stimulus, to touch on the defensive side of hostile reactions to ourselves, and to connect hostility to anxiety [p. 34].

That a patient's associations not manifestly about the transference do have a hidden transference meaning in many in-

---

[1] Lest the reader infer that the failure to make the interpretation in this session was characteristic of this analysis, I add that interpretations similar to the one suggested *were* made in this analysis on a number of occasions on the basis of similar associations. My point here is not to characterize the analysis but only to illustrate what I mean by interpretation of resistance to the awareness of transference.

stances is recognized by all analysts. Any report of analytic material of any duration is likely to include an example of how the patient's description of his relationship with someone else was used as the basis for an interpretation that this carried an implicit reference to something in his relationship with the analyst. A central point of this monograph is how ubiquitous this phenomenon is and how consistently the analyst should seek and interpret it.

2

TRANSFERENCE AND RESISTANCE

Freud often said that an analysis must centrally take account of both transference and resistance. Though my emphasis is primarily on the transference, I am obliged to discuss the relation between transference and resistance. I do so first by examining the relationships often referred to in our literature by a triad of terms—"transference," "resistance," and "defense." I then propose that if the unwarranted equation of defense and resistance is abandoned, it follows that all resistance manifests itself by way of transference.

There is a good deal of unclarity in our literature, both conceptually and terminologically, about the relation between transference and resistance. The phrases "resistance to the awareness of transference" and "resistance to the resolution of transference," which I used in the preceding chapter, do not have common currency. The expressions most commonly found in our literature are "transference resistance," "defense transference," "transference of defense," and "defense against the transference."

A review of the literature with an eye to specifying how various authors use these various terms is more confusing than clarifying. Tartakoff (1956) makes this same point in declaring that "the lack of precise differentiation between defenses against the transference neurosis and the resistance which arises as the result of transference repetition has led to endless confusion on the part of students and unnecessary controversy on the part of writers from some deviant schools" (p. 322).

Given these ambiguities, I shall focus on how I believe the various terms relate to my distinction between resistance to the awareness of transference and resistance to the resolution of transference. I suggest that the three terms which include a ref-

29

erence to defense—"defense transference," "transference of defense," and "defense against the transference"—come under resistance to the awareness of transference, while "transference resistance" conveys resistance to the resolution of transference. The only one of these terms which has currency in Freud's writings is "transference resistance." I believe that fact is related to the major contention of this monograph, namely, that resistance to the awareness of transference is underplayed both in Freud's writing and practice *and* in contemporary psychoanalysis.

TRANSFERENCE OF WISH AND TRANSFERENCE OF DEFENSE

While any manifestation of transference entails some combination of impulse and defense, spontaneously explicit manifestations of transference are likely to be thought of as impulse-driven, in contrast to implicit manifestations, which are more likely to be thought of as defensive. To be sure, the distinction between transference of wish and transference of defense is primarily conceptual. Any particular attitude on the patient's part falls somewhere along a continuum, with emphasis principally on defense at one pole and on wish at the other. Nevertheless, by and large, we can say that if the patient is not talking explicitly about the relationship, the defensive pole prevails, and we are likely to find resistance to involvement in the transference or resistance to awareness of the transference. On the other hand, if the patient is talking about the relationship explicitly, transference of wish predominates, and we are likely to describe the situation as one of resistance to resolution of the transference.

The contrast between transference of defense and transference of wish can be traced in our literature. Although the transference of defense is mentioned in Freud's paper on "The Dynamics of Transference" (1912a), it is not yet labeled as such. His very division of transference into erotic and hostile manifestations, however, testifies to an emphasis on wish. Racker (1968) clarifies this point in comparing Freud's focus here on resistance to the resolution of transference to his focus in *Beyond the Pleasure Principle* (1920a) on resistance to involvement in the transference (p. 24).

It is Anna Freud's *The Ego and the Mechanisms of Defense* (1936), however, that makes explicit the transference of defense, as opposed to that of impulse. Glover (1955) is also clear on the distinction between transference of wish and transference of defense. He believes that transference manifestations need to be looked at from two perspectives: in terms of (1) how "they enable us to recognise or reconstruct infantile instinctual development" and (2) how "the transference-resistances enable us to recognise or reconstruct the infantile ego's defensive reactions against these impulses" (p. 154). Here one might compare Fenichel's comment: "The remobilization of old anxieties upon the threat of such an eruption [of the id] brings about in the transference a repetition not only of the instinct but also of the specific defense" (1938–1939, p. 71).

The three expressions "defense transference," "transference of defense," and "defense against the transference" seem to be distinguished as different degrees of defense. If the transference is being massively resisted, the situation is likely to be pictured as defense against the transference. If, however, the transference is primarily defensive, the situation will probably be described as a defense transference. Finally, a more isolated manifestation of defense in the transference is likely to be depicted as the transference of defense.

Daniels (1969) distinguishes what he calls "defense transference" from "defense against the transference" in the context of early manifestations of transference. His definition of "defense transference" follows what I believe is fairly common usage; he sees it as habitual modes of character adaptation. . . brought into the analysis to defend against the experiencing of the more complex and more threatening transference neurosis" (p. 1000). Defense against the transference results more from "stress. . . primarily from outside, [it] concerns an immediate demand, and is a simple unit of response" (p. 1000). Defense against the transference, then, is a denial of any involvement with the analyst at all, while defense transference entails the use of habitual modes of relating to avoid a specific new encounter. I shall return to the latter issue in distinguishing transference and transference neurosis in Chapter 5.

When Tartakoff (1956) refers to "the role played by defense in preventing the development of transference manifestations" (p. 329), she is probably referring to what Daniels calls defense transference. The resistance to the awareness of transference which I have described is a more general concept, applying both to the resistance to the awareness of transference manifestations which are habitual modes of relating, that is, defense transference, and resistance to the awareness of transference manifestations of the transference neurosis, defined as nonhabitual responses arising specifically toward the analyst as a result of the preceding analytic work. (This particular distinction may not be clear in our literature because the habitual modes of relating are more likely to be present in awareness than are the manifestations of the transference neurosis.)

Tartakoff's use of "transference resistance" and the equivalent "resistance which arises as the result of transference repetition" is the same as my "resistance to the resolution of transference." Again, my term is more general since it refers to the resistance to the resolution of both transference of defense and transference of wish. The transference of defense fits Tartakoff's "resistance which arises as the result of transference repetition." Yet, strictly speaking, from this perspective defense transference is also a resistance to the resolution of transference. One thus arrives at the apparently paradoxical formulation that the transference of defense is a defense against transference. In other words, the transference of defense is a defense against transference of wish.

I suggest the phrase "resistance to involvement in the transference" for what Daniels has called "defense against the transference" because it seems to me more clearly descriptive of the phenomenon in question. I distinguish, then, three kinds of relation between transference and resistance: resistance to the awareness of transference, resistance to the resolution of transference, and resistance to involvement in transference.

RESISTANCE AND DEFENSE

Up to now I have been discussing the relation between transference and resistance and between transference of wish and transference of defense. One reason for the confusion in terminology and concepts here is the general unclarity about the relation between resistance and defense. We usually take it for granted that resistance can be expressed either by way of defense or by way of transference. I disagree with this assumption and will argue that resistance can be expressed only in the transference. Strachey (1934) comes very close to saying just that: "But, it is, of course, one of the characteristics of a resistance that it arises in relation to the analyst; and thus the interpretation of a resistance will almost inevitably be a transference interpretation" (p. 36).

This is not Freud's position, however. He gives priority to the interpretation of resistance (which is not further specified) and considers that one need deal with the transference only if the resistance has become lodged there. In *Beyond the Pleasure Principle* (1920a, p. 18), for instance, he notes that at one time the main emphasis was on the patient's resistances. The analyst then attempted to uncover these, indicating them to the patient and "inducing" him to give them up. (Here Freud specifically points to the role of "suggestion operating as 'transference.' ") Freud, however, goes on to state that this method was not completely effective since some of the repressed material could not be remembered and was enacted in the transference instead. The implication seems clear that the resistances which had to be uncovered were not being expressed in the transference.

Further evidence that Freud does not see resistance as expressed only in the transference lies close to hand. In *Inhibitions, Symptoms and Anxiety* (1926a), transference resistance is only one of the five kinds of resistance enumerated, the other four being id resistance, ego resistance (of which transference resistance is a subcategory), superego resistance, and resistance growing out of the "gain from illness" or secondary gain (pp. 159–160).

Yet elsewhere Freud says something very close to the idea that resistance is expressed only in the transference:

> When anything in the. . . subject-matter of the complex. . . is suitable for being transferred on to the figure of the doctor, that transference is carried out; it produces the next association, and announces itself by indications of a resistance—by a stoppage, for instance. We infer from this experience that the transference-idea has pene-

trated into consciousness in front of any other possible associations *because* it satisfies the resistance. . . . Over and over again, when we come near to a pathogenic complex, the portion of that complex which is capable of transference is first pushed forward into consciousness and defended with the greatest obstinacy [1912a, pp. 103–104].

Two emendations of this statement are required to come to the formulation that resistance is always expressed via transference. The first — which I shall argue in the next chapter — is that *all* aspects of the "complex" are capable of transference and do manifest themselves in the transference because there is no limit to the disguise which can take place. The second is that the transference idea does not have to be in *consciousness*. Again, what is underemphasized is that it may be present only as an allusion indicated by the extra-transference associations that do appear in consciousness. In his autobiography of 1925, Freud writes that when the transference "has become passionate or has been converted into hostility, it becomes the principal tool of the resistance" (p. 42). Here, too, then, Freud seems to believe that, at least for some periods of an analysis, the only transference present is facilitating transference and the resistance is expressed otherwise than in the transference. As I shall discuss in the next chapter, this idea implies a model of the therapeutic process in which the analysis of the transference is ancillary to, not coterminous with, the analysis of the neurosis.

Before discussing the reconceptualization of resistance I have in mind, it will be useful to review some of the major milestones in the writing on technique for opinions on where the resistance is primarily to be found. It can be shown that though the idea that resistance is always expressed in the transference is approached, it is not directly stated, except by Strachey (1934).

Wilhelm Reich (1933) inaugurated a major chapter in psychoanalytic technique by arguing that resistance is primarily lodged in the character and that the therapist's interpretations should first be directed to that resistance. Although various objections have been appropriately raised to Reich's recommendation, they are not put as I would put it — namely, that Reich describes character as a defense in *intrapsychic* terms and fails to see that this defense is available for interpretation *only* as it is ex-

pressed *interpersonally* in the transference. The distinction I am
proposing here is between "defense" as connoting something intrapsychic and "resistance" as connoting something interpersonal. In other words, character defense has concomitant expressions in the transference; these are the *resistances*, which, in my
opinion, should receive priority in interpretation.

In his article "Concerning the Theory of Psychoanalytic
Technique" (1935), Fenichel offers several formulas for what
should take precedence in interpretation and at times criticizes
the technical recommendations of Reich. He implies that these
several formulas are different ways of saying the same thing:
that the affect, what lies on the surface, and resistance go together. Citing Reich's views, Fenichel indicates his agreement
that the analyst should look for affect in "characterological behavior" (p. 452). He does not dispute Reich's view that the character manifestations are resistances nor that priority should be
given to these "frozen resistances" in the character. Nonetheless,
he does believe one should first collect as much information
about the patient as possible because "the more *information* one
has, the better armed one goes into the actual struggle with the
resistances" (p. 454).

Anna Freud (1936), however, attacks Reich's recommendation on the very grounds that the affect is *not* available in the frozen character resistances. She argues that Reich tackles the defense at an inappropriate place, at a point where remnants from
past defensive activities "have become dissociated from their
original situations" and fixed into particular character traits. Instead, the battle should be waged at a point where there is "a
present conflict between ego, instinct, and affect" (p. 33). She
does not specify, however, whether the "present conflict" should
be dealt with within or outside of the transference and thus fails
to question explicitly whether these character manifestations are
appropriately called resistances (though she does refer to them
as *defensive*).

Kaiser's (1934) view is similar to that of Anna Freud. He distinguishes character resistance from transference resistance in
phenomenological terms, emphasizing its impersonal appearance and its lack of "affective vitality" (p. 398). Yet he, too, fails
to question the designation "resistance."

While Sterba (1953) decidedly looks askance at Reich's implicit equation of transference and resistance, this is not because he questions the appropriateness of calling character manifestations "resistance." His objection is rather to Reich's suspiciousness of every positive transference manifestation from the very beginning of treatment (p. 5).

In criticizing Reich, Fenichel does say at one point that priority goes to transference interpretation. This conclusion follows from his objections to Reich's aggressive way of "shattering the armor plating," which Sterba also takes exception to. Fenichel points out: "The conviction that a consistent working through of character resistance is the one and only correct method may make one overlook the fact that experiencing this kind of analysis may itself become for the patient a *transference resistance*. This would naturally be an even more superficial one than the 'character resistance' and would have to be dealt with first" (1935, p. 456). Here Fenichel comes close to recognizing that resistance means something in the ongoing interaction, that is, in the transference. It will be recalled that I indicated in my Introduction that if one finds that the patient is experiencing the interpretation of the transference as an aggression, that experience has priority of interpretation.

Glover (1955) goes somewhat further than Fenichel. He recommends interpretation of a character *reaction* in *the transference*, at least in the case of a paranoiac character. Designating three major character reactions in the paranoiac individual—"suspicion, sensitiveness to contact and a defensive aggressiveness"— Glover argues that suspicion has the first claim to attention. And here Glover adds that "also from the *first* session the transference aspects should be raised in a slightly indirect form of ventilating the patient's reaction to treatment" (p. 252). The reference seems to be to what is called defense transference. Glover's remarks in this context may be generalized to the principle that the patient's habitual modes of relating should have priority of interpretation even when they appear as allusions rather than explicitly in the transference—presuming due consideration for the patient's ability to tolerate the interpretation.

My criticisms of Reich can be summarized by saying that he fails to recognize that the character can be dealt with as the presenting surface and presenting affect only insofar as it is discernible in the transference. He also fails to recognize the repercussions on the transference of the analyst's interpretations of the transference. Nor does he see the difference between facilitating transference and transference employed as resistance; instead, he deals with all transference as if it were only resistance.

Here one should mention that Kaiser (1934) goes so far as to insist that *no* content but *only* resistance interpretations should be made. An offshoot of his view is that an effective interpretation of resistance can be recognized in the fact that the patient can barely restrain himself from acting out the impulse which the resistance has been directed against. Criticizing Kaiser, Fenichel (1935) again comes close to recognizing that resistance is expressed only in transference. He argues that while the formerly repressed impulses "must be *experienced* as actually existing (and, as, at the moment, inappropriate — as in the 'transference') ...they need not for this reason be acted out" (p. 461).

The authors cited state that priority of interpretation should variously go to where the affect lies, to the present conflict, to the character, and to the resistance. The transference is accorded priority only if that is where the presenting resistance lies. As I suggested above, the inference is that there are resistances other than transference resistance. It is this conclusion I disagree with. In my opinion, there is a confusion here between the concepts of resistance and defense. I would argue that defense is an intrapsychic concept while resistance is an interpersonal one. It is therefore logical to see resistance as expressible only in the transference, that is, in the way in which the intrapsychic formations actually become expressed in the analytic situation.

The confusion between defense as an intrapsychic concept and resistance as an interpersonal manifestation in the analytic situation began with Freud. This becomes clear in reviewing Freud's (1926a) way of articulating the relation between the ego as a source of resistance and the three consequent manifestations, with their differing dynamics. The first ego resistance Freud names is *"repression* resistance" (p. 160).[1] He then goes on

---

[1] A few pages later, Freud proposes to revert to his earlier designation of repression as one of the defenses. Had he kept to this classification, he would have spoken here of defense resistance rather than repression resistance.

to explain "*transference* resistance," which he sees as similar in nature but with "different and much clearer effects in analysis, since it succeeds in establishing a relation to the analytic situation or the analyst himself and thus re-animating a repression which should only have been recollected" (p. 160). The implication is that while transference resistance is expressed in relation to the analytic situation, repression resistance is expressed only in relation to a recollection. It does not succeed in establishing a relation to the analytic situation or the analyst himself, nor does it become a reanimation of a repression — that is, it does not find current expression in the transference, whether in ideation or action. My argument is that to say that there is a resistance is equivalent to saying that it *does* find such expression.

That Freud confused intrapsychic and interpersonal concepts in his conceptualization of resistance is even clearer in his enumeration of the remaining kinds of resistances: the ego resistance of secondary gain and the id and superego resistances. I believe that here Freud is describing the various *sources* of resistance, rather than its actual manifestations in the analytic situation. His inclusion of transference resistance among the types of resistance is thus misleading, for the transference is not a source of resistance but the vehicle of its expression.

In reconsidering Freud's classification of resistances, Fenichel (1938–1939) concludes that all resistances are essentially ego resistance, except id resistance. And even the id, he argues, can be influenced only by way of the ego (pp. 33–34, 82–83).

But my revision is more radical than this. My contention is that the concept of resistance should be restricted to what takes place in relation to the interpersonal analytic interaction. This conclusion is in line with the thrust of Stone's (1973) formulation. He stresses the primary importance of establishing "a viable scientific and working concept of resistance to the therapeutic process as a manifestation of a reactivated intrapsychic conflict in a new interpersonal context" (p. 43).

Yet Stone follows Freud's broad definition of resistance as "*whatever interrupts the progress of analytic work*" (1900, p. 517).[2] As Freud himelf explains in a later footnote, even an external im-

---

[2] This sentiment is reechoed in Freud's labeling "all the forces that oppose the work of recovery as the patient's 'resistances' " (1926b, p. 223).

pediment is implied in this statement, insofar as the resistance determines how the external impediment is dealt with. Similarly, Stone (1973, p. 46) agrees with Glover's argument that any mental function can be used for defensive purposes "*and hence give rise during the analysis to the phenomena of resistance*" (1955, p. 57). My point is to make very clear that these statements refer to the sources of resistance and not to its expression.

Freud's view that resistance could be expressed in other ways, as well as in the transference, is clearly stated in one of his last writings, "Analysis Terminable and Interminable" (1937a). In commenting that no transference analogous to the male's rebellious overcompensation for homosexuality can arise from the female's wish for a penis, Freud adds that this also shows us that the manifest form resistance takes — whether transference or not — is immaterial. What is crucial for him is that "the resistance prevents any change from taking place" (p. 252).

Yet Freud's earliest accounts of resistance do anchor it firmly in the interpersonal treatment situation. In *Studies on Hysteria* (Breuer and Freud, 1893–1895), he writes of his discovery that with his insistence new recollections by the patient would emerge. The need for this effort on his part led him to surmise that what he had to overcome was a resistance: "*by means of my psychical work I had to overcome a psychical force in the patients which was opposed to the pathogenic ideas becoming conscious (being remembered)*" (p. 268). In attempting to focus the patient's attention on an idea that was clearly incompatible with the patient's ego, Freud recognized "in the form of *resistance*...the same force as had shown itself in the form of *repulsion* [called "defense" a moment before] when the symptom was generated" (p. 269). Resistance is the interpersonal manifestation of defense.

"How does it come about that transference is so admirably suited to be a means of resistance?" asks Freud (1912a, p. 104). So admirably suited, I might add, that the analysis of resistance is in effect the analysis of transference. What Freud proposes as the answer, however, is not always clearly recognized because his first reply steps aside from the main issue somewhat to make the distinction between facilitating and obstructing transference. He claims that the transference "is suitable for resistance to the treatment only in so far as it is a negative transference or a positive transference of repressed erotic impulses" (1912a, p. 105). And it is here that he distinguishes the unobjectionable positive transference as a conscious attachment which is the "vehicle of success" in analytic treatment (see p. 10).

Freud's direct response to the question actually appears at the end of the essay. To show that this is indeed his reply, I shall quote at some length from the text. Freud begins, "In all these reflections, however, we have hitherto dealt only with one side of the phenomenon of transference; we must turn our attention to another aspect of the same subject" (p. 107). He then describes how a patient under the sway of transference resistance ignores the real situation.[3] In seeking for an explanation for this impression, Freud finds that the factors involved "arise once again from the psychological situation in which the treatment places the patient" (p. 107).

> The unconscious impulses do not want to be remembered in the way the treatment desires them to be, but endeavour to reproduce themselves in accordance with the timelessness of the unconscious and its capacity for hallucination. Just as happens in dreams, the patient regards the products of the awakening of his unconscious impulses as contemporaneous and real; he seeks to put his passions into action without taking any account of the real situation [as above (fn. 3), I differ]. The doctor tries to compel him to fit these emotional impulses into the nexus of the treatment and of his life-history, to submit them to intellectual consideration and to understand them in the light of their psychical value [p. 108].

It is because the patient attempts to enact his impulses in the interpersonal interaction with the analyst that the resistance is interpersonally expressed, that is, *in* the transference.

Bordin (1974) also makes this point. He declares that *"most of the critical interpretations of the resistance are also interpretations of transference,"* as the conflict-laden wishes center on early parental objects. *"Moreover,"* he continues, *"since the modes of defense are grounded in this interpersonal context, they are interpersonal in character, creating the situation that most resistances will take a transference form"* (p. 11).

I would go further, to say that *all*, not merely most, interpre-

---

[3] Later I shall argue that the patient does *not* ignore the real situation but takes account of it as plausibly as he can. This should, then, be recognized in the analyst's interpretation.

tations of resistance are transference interpretations. Many interpretations that are called interpretations of resistance are in fact interpretations of defense, that is, they are intrapsychic, not interpersonal interpretations. It may be that the recognition that all resistance interpretations are interpersonal interpretations has been obscured by a fear that to do so would commit oneself to an interpersonal rather than an intrapsychic view of human psychology. But one need not be driven into such a dichotomy. Intrapsychic conflicts can find interpersonal expression in the analytic situation. Nor does the recognition that this is so mean one is espousing the view that development is solely determined by interpersonal factors. Biological givens, in their psychological representation, enter into development as independent factors, but the ultimate outcome of the interaction of givens and environmental factors is the intrapsychic formation which becomes interpersonally expressed in human interaction.

3

CENTRALITY OF
THE ANALYSIS OF TRANSFERENCE

FREUD'S VIEWS

The analysis of the transference is both the heart of analytic technique as well as its most difficult aspect. This point is so taken for granted among psychoanalysts that it would seem unnecessary to document it. Freud himself states this opinion unequivocally: the "handling [of the transference] remains the most difficult as well as the most important part of the technique of analysis" (1925, p. 43). Elsewhere he explains that the most demanding requirements for analytic technique arise when the analyst must "convince the patient that he is not in love but only obliged to stage a revival of an old piece" (1926b, p. 227). It is here, Freud argues, that the most serious mistakes and the "greatest successes" occur. "It would be folly to attempt to evade the difficulties by suppressing or neglecting the transference; whatever else had been done in the treatment, it would not deserve the name of analysis" (p. 227).

As Bergmann and Hartman (1976) point out in their collection of papers on analytic technique, "some analysts tend to favor a model of the analyst as an observer and purveyor of interpretation, while others rely more on what they learn from the interaction itself" (p. 5). While these authors note Freud's (1914) interest in "the possibility of translating the original neurosis into a transference neurosis," they believe he represents the first model. I agree that this is correct for Freud's *practice* and shall deal with the evidence for that in Chapter 10. Here, however, I wish to show that in writing about the *theory* of technique Freud proposed both models at differing times.

43

To articulate the models from a slightly different angle: in one, the transference is primarily seen as a resistance to the recovery of memories and the therapeutic gain results primarily from the recovery of these memories. In the other, the transference is primarily a result of the patient's effort to realize his wishes and the therapeutic gain results primarily from reexperiencing these wishes in the transference, realizing that they are significantly determined by something preexisting within the patient, and experiencing something new in examining them together with the analyst — the one to whom the wishes are now directed.

I shall begin by offering illustrations of Freud's statement of the first model, in which the transference is primarily understood as a resistance to the recovery of memories and in which the goal of analysis is to recover these memories. In this model emphasis is on the search for genetic material as such and on genetic transference interpretations. In his paper on "Remembering, Repeating and Working-Through" (1914), after reviewing earlier analytic techniques and concluding that the art of interpretation consists mainly in recognizing the resistances present on the surface of the patient's mind, Freud writes: "The aim of these different techniques has, of course, remained the same. Descriptively speaking, it is to fill in gaps in memory; dynamically speaking, it is to overcome resistances due to repression" (pp. 147–148). Later in the same paper he reiterates that "while the patient experiences his illness as something real and contemporary, we have to do our therapeutic work on it, which consists in a large measure in tracing it back to the past" (p. 152).

That Freud continued to regard the filling in of gaps in memory as crucial to the analytic process may be seen in "Constructions in Analysis" (1937b), one of the few late works devoted primarily to technique. Yet even in that paper, his faithful adherence to his clinical experience may be seen in his admission that "Quite often we do not succeed in bringing the patient to recollect what has been repressed," despite the patient's conviction that a reconstruction which the analyst has made is correct (p. 265).

It seems very unlikely here that Freud simply means that the recovery of the past has a therapeutic effect. That would be no more than a restatement of the cathartic theory of therapy, according to which the therapeutic effect is due to the discharge of the "strangulated affect" associated with the repressed memory. He must mean, rather, that the recovery of the memory plays an important role in the resolution of the transference since it provides an explanation for how the transference comes to be. In other words, the recovery of the past is shorthand for genetic transference interpretation and is in all likelihood a sign that the transference has been successfully resolved rather than being the therapeutic agent itself.

I now turn to several statements in which Freud's emphasis on the importance of remembering the past is balanced by an emphasis on that part of the work which takes place in the analytic situation itself. He says, for example, that if the resistances have been adequately dealt with, the memories of the past can be obtained with relative ease. This point is made twice in the paper on "Remembering, Repeating and Working-Through" (1914). First he indicates that when the resistances "have been got the better of, the patient often relates the forgotten situations and connections without any difficulty" (p. 147). Later he comments: "From the repetitive reactions which are exhibited in the transference we are led along the familiar paths to the awakening of the memories, which appear without difficulty, as it were, after the resistance has been overcome" (pp. 154–155). So, too, in his "Observations on Transference-Love" (1915), he describes how, after the patient has become aware of the detailed characteristics of her state of being in love, "she will herself open the way to the infantile roots of her love" (p. 166).

Another passage clarifying Freud's emphasis on the experience in the transference may be found in the lecture on transference in the *Introductory Lectures*, and bears repeating here. Freud explains that once the treatment takes over, the patient's illness becomes focused on "a single point—his relation to the doctor. . . . When the transference has risen to this significance, work upon the patient's memories retreats far into the background. Thereafter it is not incorrect to say that we are no longer concerned with the patient's earlier illness but with a newly created and transformed neurosis which has taken the former's place"

(1916–1917, p. 444). Later, in the same essay, he writes that the repression process is only in part revised through the recovery of the related memories. The "decisive" work, Freud claims, takes place through the creation in the transference of "new editions of the old conflicts." In this way, "the transference becomes the battlefield on which all the mutually struggling forces should meet one another" (p. 454).

The oscillation between emphasis on memories and on impulses, which characterizes Freud's work almost from the beginning (Rapaport, 1958), may be seen in this issue too. I have already quoted his (1914) remark that the goal of the analytic process is to fill the gaps in memory. But in the same paper he comments: "Only when the resistance is at its height can the analyst, working in common with his patient, discover the repressed instinctual impulses which are feeding the resistance; and it is this kind of experience which convinces the patient of the existence and power of such impulses" (p. 155).

Indeed, this passage clarifies what the transference resistance is a resistance against. Its emphasis differs from Freud's sometimes-stated view that the transference is a resistance against remembering. It is consistent, rather, with Freud's explanation of why the transference is so admirably suited to serve the resistance (as I discussed earlier). Here we see that this is so because the patient's impulses continue to seek enactment in the present. The resistance, then, is to abandoning the search for the gratification of these impulses. One of Freud's great achievements is his demonstration that whatever a person's childhood experiences, his own wishes play a major role in how he interprets them. If the therapist's emphasis falls on the memories of the past, there is the danger that the emphasis will be on the events of the past rather than on how the patient's wishes led him to construe these events. Even if the emphasis is on the wishes, their reconstruction lacks the immediacy and more certain knowledge of their character which accompanies experiencing them in the transference.

Freud's two different positions also find expression in the two very different ways in which he speaks of the transference. In the same paper (1912a), he refers to the transference, on the one hand, as *"the most powerful resistance* to the treatment" (p. 101)

and, on the other, as "making the patient's. . . impulses immediate and manifest. For when all is said and done, it is impossible
to destroy anyone *in absentia* or *in effigie*" (p. 108).

In addition, these two views are strikingly evident in two de-
scriptions of the phases of an analysis. Freud writes: "In the
first, all the libido is forced from the symptoms into the transference and concentrated there; in the second, the struggle is waged
around this new object and the libido is liberated from it" (1916–
1917, p. 455). A few years later (1920b), he notes that the analyst begins by unfolding to the patient "the reconstruction of the
genesis of his disorder as deduced from the material brought up
in the analysis." The next stage involves the patient's remembering as much as possible of the repressed past and attempting
"to repeat the rest as if he were in some way living it over again"
(p. 152).

I shall now try to demonstrate that the model of the analysis
of the transference as the avenue to the analysis of the neurosis
can be derived from several points made in Freud's writings,
partly explicitly and partly implicitly. Freud indicates that:
(1) the resistance is primarily expressed by repetition: (2) the
repetition takes place both within and outside the analytic situation, but the analyst seeks to deal with it primarily within the
analytic situation; (3) the repetition can take place not only in
the motor sphere (through action) but also in the psychical
sphere; and (4) the psychical sphere is not confined to remembering but includes the present as well.

Freud's emphasis that the purpose of resistance is to prevent
remembering may obscure his point that resistance shows itself
primarily — I would say entirely — by repetition, whether inside
or outside the analytic situation. "The greater the resistance," he
remarks, "the more extensively will acting out (repetition) replace remembering" (1914, p. 151). Similarly, in "The Dynamics of Transference" (1912a), Freud insists that the main reason
the transference is so well suited to serve the resistance is that
the "unconscious impulses do not want to be remembered. . .
but endeavour to reproduce themselves" (p. 108). He sees the
transference as a resistance primarily insofar as it is a repetition.

I now wish to restate this point in terms of the relation between transference and resistance. I have just noted that the re-

sistance expresses itself in repetition, that is, in transference both inside and outside the analytic situation. To deal with the transference therefore is equivalent to dealing with the resistance. Freud's emphasis on the transference within the analytic situation is so strong that it has come to mean only the repetition within the analytic situation, even though conceptually speaking repetition outside the analytic situation is also transference. At one point Freud himself uses the term in this second sense: "We soon perceive that the transference is itself only a piece of repetition, and that the repetition is a transference of the forgotten past not only on to the doctor but also on to all the other aspects of the current situation. We... find... the compulsion to repeat, which now replaces the impulsion to remember, not only in his personal attitude to his doctor but also in every other activity and relationship which may occupy his life at the time" (1914, p. 151).

It is important to realize that Freud holds that the expansion of the repetition inside the analytic situation, whether or not in a reciprocal relationship to repetition outside the analytic situation, is the avenue to controlling the repetition. He states: "The main instrument... for curbing the patient's compulsion to repeat and for turning it into a motive for remembering lies in the handling of the transference. We render the compulsion harmless, and indeed useful, by giving it the right to assert itself in a definite field" (1914, p. 154).

Kanzer has discussed this issue well in his paper on "The Motor Sphere of the Transference" (1966). He writes of the "double-pronged stick-and-carrot" technique by which the transference is fostered within the analytic situation and discouraged outside the analytic situation. The "stick" is the principle of abstinence, as exemplified in the admonition against making important decisions during treatment, and the "carrot" is the opportunity afforded the transference to expand within the treatment "in almost complete freedom" as on a "playground" (Freud, 1914, p. 154).[1]

As Freud himself puts it: "Provided only that the patient shows

[1] A more exact translation might have a less friendly tone since *Tummelplatz* means "arena, wrestling ground, or place of combat."

compliance enough to respect the necessary conditions of the analysis, we regularly succeed in giving all the symptoms of the illness a new transference meaning and in replacing his ordinary neurosis by a 'transference-neurosis' of which he can be cured by the therapeutic work" (1914, p. 154).

The reason it is desirable for the transference to be expressed within the treatment is that there it is always within reach of our intervention (1914, p. 154). In a later statement Freud makes the same point. He stresses that with this "new edition" of the illness — the transference neurosis — the analyst can follow its course from the beginning and take note of its origin and growth. Moreover, "we are especially well able to find our way about in it since, as its object, we are situated at its very centre" (1916–1917, p. 444). Freud's formulation here implies that the expansion of the transference in the treatment situation is spontaneous, but in fact the analytic situation and the analyst's interpretations actively bring about this expansion.

Freud emphasizes the *acting* out of the repetition in the transference so strongly that one may overlook that repetition in the transference does not necessarily mean it is *enacted* in gross motor terms. Enactment can also be expressed in attitudes, feelings, and intentions. Indeed, the repetition often does take one of these forms rather than motor action. Such repetition is in the psychical rather than the motor sphere.

The importance of making this clear is that Freud may be mistakenly read to mean that repetition in the psychical sphere can only mean remembering the past. For instance, such a misinterpretation might arise with Freud's statement that the analyst must struggle "to keep in the psychical sphere all the impulses which the patient would like to direct into the motor sphere; and he celebrates it as a triumph for the treatment if he can bring it about that something the patient wishes to discharge in action is disposed of through the work of remembering" (1914, p. 153). It is true that when the patient's repetition lies in the motor sphere the analyst attempts to convert it into the psychical sphere, but transference may be in the psychical sphere to begin with, albeit disguised. The repetition in the psychical sphere includes enactment in the transference as well as remembering.

I conclude that because of the resistance to the awareness of transference, the transference has to be disguised. When the disguise is unmasked by interpretation, it becomes clear that despite the inevitable differences between outside situations and the transference situation, the content is the same for the purpose of the analytic work. Therefore the analysis of the transference and the analysis of the neurosis coincide. In other words, the transference is analyzed not for its own sake but in the effort to overcome the neurosis. As I noted above, Freud sees the mastering of the transference neurosis as coinciding with "getting rid of the illness which was originally brought to the treatment" (1916–1917, p. 444).

Even if we grant the unique effectiveness of transference interpretation in contrast to extra-transference interpretation, the question remains of whether the patient's neurosis is entirely duplicated in the transference. The issue is not whether every detail of the neurosis is duplicated in the transference but whether the significant aspects which need to be dealt with are. To the extent that they are not, interpretations have to be outside the transference.

In "Analysis Terminable and Interminable" (1937a), Freud indicates that significant conflicts may not appear in the transference because they are no longer active in the patient's current life. But another opinion of his casts more serious doubts on whether the transference neurosis precisely duplicates the content of the preexisting neurosis. In "The Dynamics of Transference" (1912a), Freud underlines that as one approaches the "pathogenic complex," the part that "is capable of transference is first pushed forward into consciousness and defended with the greatest obstinacy" (p. 104). But he adds a footnote explaining that one should not therefore assume that the part chosen for this display of resistance has particular pathogenic significance: "If in the course of a battle there is a particularly embittered struggle over the possession of some little church or some individual farm, there is no need to suppose that the church is a national shrine, perhaps, or that the house shelters the army's paychest. The value of the object may be a purely tactical one and may perhaps emerge only in this one battle" (p. 104n). The same point is made in the *Introductory Lectures* (1916–1917, pp.

455–456). One might conclude, then, that the content of the transference neurosis by no means comprehensively duplicates the content of the preexisting neurosis.

I believe that Freud may have failed to recognize how distorted a version of the original pathogenic issue the manifest transference may be. Were the transference brought *fully* into awareness, it might become apparent that the issues in the transference were indeed the issues of the preexisting neurosis. Such a conclusion would be consistent with Freud's view that all the symptoms of the illness acquire a meaning in the transference, and that when the transference has been resolved, so has the neurosis which brought the patient to treatment (see my earlier quotation on p. 49). As we have seen, Freud himself describes "the transference as a playground...in which [the compulsion to repeat] is expected to display to us everything in the way of pathogenic instinct that is hidden in the patient's mind" (1914, p. 154).

In summary, Freud's theory clearly argues that the work of analysis consists in encouraging the transference to expand as much as possible within the analytic situation because it is most accurately known and most effectively dealt with there. Insofar as possible, the transference replaces the original neurosis, and with the resolution of the transference comes the concomitant resolution of the original neurosis. Freud asserts that the more closely this ideal is approached, the more effective is the therapy.

OTHER AUTHORS' VIEWS ON TRANSFERENCE

I shall not attempt a comprehensive review of the changing fortunes of the principle of the centrality and priority of the transference in analytic work. Instead, I shall confine myself to a few outstanding landmarks.

To begin with, Ferenczi and Rank (1923) have argued for a greater emphasis on "experiencing in the transference," as compared with the practice of their time. Their book has been attacked for failing to recognize the necessity of working through (e.g., Alexander, 1925).[2] In their zeal to combat what they con-

---

[2] It is of interest that Alexander later changed his mind and used the book as a point of departure for his own proposals to manipulate the transference (Alexander, French, et al., 1946).

sider intellectualization, Ferenczi and Rank do seem to play down the importance of genetic interpretations, though they explicitly write of the need to relate the transference to the past. What they highlight, however, is the need to analyze the repercussions on the transference of the actual analytic situation.

The paper analysts are most likely to think of in considering the centrality of the transference is Strachey's "The Nature of the Therapeutic Action of Psycho-Analysis" (1934). It is in this paper that Strachey introduces the phrase "mutative interpretation," meaning an interpretation that brings about a change. Strachey confronts the question directly by asking: "Is it to be understood that no extra-transference interpretation can set in motion the chain of events which I have suggested as being the essence of psycho-analytic therapy?" (p. 34). He replies in the affirmative, adding that one of the main intentions of his paper is to make explicit "the dynamic distinctions between transference and extra-transference interpretations."

Actually Strachey retreats a bit from this unequivocal position that only transference interpretations are mutative. Instead of saying that extra-transference interpretations *cannot* be mutative, he notes they are not usually "given at the point of urgency" (p. 34). Similarly, he states that, in extra-transference interpretation, it is not impossible but only more difficult for the patient to see clearly the distinction between what is real in the situation and what is fantasy. In these respects, then, "an extra-transference interpretation is liable to be both less effective and more risky than a transference one" (p. 34).

Nor is Strachey against all extra-transference interpretation. He in fact believes that through an extra-transference interpretation, "the analyst can provoke a situation in the transference of which he can then give a mutative interpretation" (pp. 37–38). While this is true, I would argue that extra-transference interpretations are not necessary to provoke such situations in the transference. Not only are these situations inevitably and ubiquitously present, but transference interpretations can also provoke them.

Strachey goes on to claim that the majority of the interpretations that are made are extra-transference interpretations. Yet he has some difficulty in justifying this, presumably since he regards only transference interpretations as mutative. In order to clarify this imbalance, he resorts to an analogy to the battlefield. He sees "the acceptance of a transference interpretation" as "the capture of a key position." In contrast, "extra-transference interpretations correspond to the general advance and to the consolidation of a fresh line which are made possible by the capture of the key position" (p. 38). Just as in war the general advance is eventually met by a new "check," leading to "the capture of a further key position," so, too, in the analysis there is an "oscillation" between the consolidation of insight through extra-transference interpretation and new insight through transference interpretation. That my position lays even greater stress on the transference impetus will become clear in the chapters to follow.

Fenichel's (1938–1939) authoritative monograph on analytic technique appeared shortly after Strachey's paper (see Gill, 1980–1981). Although this work is clearly not intended as a comprehensive statement on technique, and although there is evidence in the monograph itself that Fenichel probably gave greater emphasis to the transference in practice than he does in his theoretical formulations, it is nevertheless noteworthy that he puts less stress on the transference than does Freud in his writings. Fenichel summarizes several technical instructions for what should receive priority in interpretation. He tells the analyst to: (1) "Work always where the patient's affect lies at the moment," (2) begin by interpreting "what is on the surface at the moment," and (3) interpret resistance before interpreting content (1935, p. 451). What is striking is that none of these formulas refers directly to the transference.

Although Fenichel describes these formulas as "transmitted by tradition from Freud," the last two at least are in fact *explicit* in Freud's writings. In reviewing the stages of the development of his technique, for example, Freud mentions that the analyst "contents himself with studying whatever is present for the time being on the surface of the patient's mind, and he employs the art of interpretation mainly for the purpose of recognizing the resistances which appear there, and making them conscious to the patient" (1914, p. 147).

In one of the other papers on technique, Freud is even more specific that the resistance must be dealt with first. But, even more important, is that he, unlike Fenichel, explicitly connects this to interpretation within the transference. As I quoted earlier (pp. 14–15), he writes that, with every communication, "we must wait until the disturbance of the transference by the successive emergence of transference-resistances has been removed" (1913, p. 144). I have already argued that in this statement the "strong" transference Freud refers to as being disturbed is the unobjectionable positive transference (the facilitating transference), while by "transference-resistances" he probably means the explicit transference, that is, resistance to the resolution of transference. What I would add is that even before this, priority of interpretation should go to the indirect allusions to the transference, to the resistance to the awareness of transference, which also "disturbs" the facilitating transference.

While Fenichel only fails to single out transference interpretation for special mention, Anna Freud (1969) criticizes what she considers to be an overemphasis on the transference in analytic work. I shall, however, defer a discussion of her views to my chapter on the Kleinian view of transference because I believe her remarks are essentially a reaction to that view.

In a discussion of the relative roles of transference and extra-transference interpretations, Sylvia Payne (1946) writes that Anna Freud, Fenichel, Edward Bibring, and other experienced analysts maintain that analyzing the drive derivatives and their correlated defenses "is as important as direct transference interpretations." She says that "an unconscious transference situation" does not "operate as a resistance unless it is a transference of a repressed imago" and unless the transference "is being relived with the analyst" (p. 14).

My criticism of this view is that "an unconscious transference situation" is always present in the analysis and should be searched for in the indirect allusions to the transference. Furthermore, since the transference in the here-and-now *is* being relived with the analyst and *is* ultimately related to a "repressed imago," Payne's formulation is not a valid argument against giving precedence to transference interpretation.

Kris (1956a) has described the interrelation of the analysis of current conflicts and the recall of the past as a "circular process," though his statement does not refer specifically to the transference. While he does not take issue with the traditional view that "the lifting of repression. . . strengthens the ego," he adds that in its turn the strengthening of the ego helps to "further reduction of anticathectic energies" (p. 82). Translated into transference terms, this view would be similar to Strachey's depiction of the oscillation between transference and extra-transference interpretations and amounts to a lesser emphasis on the transference than my position represents.

For a more recent statement of the centrality of transference analysis, I cite Stone (1973). In the context of his discussion of resistance, he clearly states that, beyond major advances in ego psychology and studies of character, the increasingly central role of transference analysis in the analytic work has greatly modified both the approach to and conceptualization of resistance. He stresses that "the transference is indeed the central dynamism of the entire psychoanalytic situation; and the transference neurosis certainly provides the one framework which gives essential and accessible configuration to the potentially panpsychic scope of free association" (p. 57).

Stone (1967, 1973), however, takes a less emphatic position on the relative roles of transference and extra-transference interpretations than I do. Even so, he underlines the importance of extra-transference material for clarification rather than interpretation as such. According to him, many analysts do not assign a unique value to transference interpretations and instead base their choice of transference or extra-transference interpretation on economic considerations. Pointing to "the necessarily 'distributed' character of a variable fraction of transference interpretation," Stone then declares that "the extra-analytic life of the patient often provides indispensable data for the understanding of detailed complexities of his psychic functioning, because of the sheer variety of its references, some of which cannot be reproduced in the relationship to the analyst" (1967, p. 35).

As examples of what cannot be reproduced in the analytic situation, Stone cites repartee, a dialogue with an angry employer, or a reaction to a real danger of dismissal. I do not see, however, why such issues cannot find affectively meaningful representation in the transference. I believe Stone's examples betray an overemphasis on the role of the external situation in determining a patient's attitudes. Instead, I suggest that even with an analyst who maintains appropriate reserve in the analytic situation, a patient can be convinced (and not entirely mistaken!) that the analyst is engaged in repartee, that he is in dialogue with an angry analyst, or in real danger of dismissal from the analysis.

With regard to the question of how comprehensively the transference neurosis can duplicate the preexisting neurosis, Stone (1967) does not believe complete duplication is possible. He argues that "the analyst, even in the strictly transference sphere, cannot be assigned all the transference roles simultaneously" (p. 33). Moreover, he claims that, quite aside from acting-out episodes, the patient's contradictory attitudes, not yet in awareness, may force him to look for other transference objects, at least before these attitudes are brought to awareness and verbalized. Stone thus concludes that "extratransference interpretations cannot be set aside, or underestimated in importance" (p. 35).

On the other hand, he raises a question about Freud's conclusion that a conflict which is dormant in the patient's life context will not appear in the transference:

> If we cannot, as Freud [1937a] pointed out, artificially mobilize a transference conflict which is dormant in the patient's life context, we may at times by tactful interpretive address to its analytic "absence," and in an affective climate which permits the patient to accept a second confrontation, to some degree mobilize the conflict which is indeed active but, because of archaic dread of the transference, moving toward delayed but severe symptomatic solution or unhappy large-scale materialization in the patient's everyday life [1973, p. 71].

Fenichel (1938–1939) questions Freud's conclusion too. He does not believe that these conflicts are completely dormant; "the ego merely acts as if they were" (p. 118). The analyst, according to him, often has to "detect" the conflict from small clues. In this case, then, he must demonstrate "to the patient the actuality of the 'conflict' " (p. 118).

The upshot of this review seems to me to be that only Strachey approaches what I think is demanded by Freud's logic — that the analysis of the transference should have overwhelming centrality in the analytic process. The remainder of this monograph (except for the historical review) is devoted to a further explication of how this can be done. The first issue to which I shall turn is how the transference is encouraged to expand within the analytic situation. Although Freud says this should be done, he offers relatively little on how it can be done.

4

HOW THE TRANSFERENCE
IS ENCOURAGED TO EXPAND
WITHIN THE ANALYTIC SITUATION

The analytic situation itself fosters the development of attitudes which significantly affect what the patient brings to the situation, i.e., his transferences. The analyst's reserve provides the patient with equivocal cues. The therapeutic context of the analytic situation engenders strong emotional responses. As Freud himself points out, the very fact that the patient has a neurosis indicates some missing satisfaction and thus it is quite understandable that this "libidinal cathexis [and I would add negative feelings],...which is held ready in anticipation, should be directed...to the figure of the doctor" (1912a, p. 100).

While the analytic setup itself fosters the expansion of the transference within the analytic situation, the interpretation of resistance to the awareness of transference can further this expansion. Contrary to the widespread belief that the existence of the analytic situation alone is enough for the transference to expand spontaneously within it, I am contending that only with the interpretation of resistance to the awareness of transference will appropriate expansion occur.

There are important resistances on the part of both the patient and the analyst to awareness of the transference. On the patient's side, the reason lies in the difficulty in recognizing erotic and hostile impulses toward the very person to whom they have to be disclosed. On the analyst's side, this resistance arises because the patient is likely to attribute to him the very attitudes that are most likely to cause him discomfort. It is often the attitudes the patient believes the analyst has toward him which the patient is least likely to voice, in a general sense because the patient feels that it is impertinent for him to concern himself with the analyst's feelings and in a more specific sense because the attitudes the patient ascribes to the analyst are often attitudes the patient feels the analyst will either not like or be uncomfortable about. It is for this reason that the analyst must be especially alert to the attitudes the patient believes the *analyst* has, not only to the attitudes the patient has.

The resistance to the awareness of these attitudes is responsible for their appearing in various disguises in the patient's manifest associations and for the analyst's reluctance to unmask these disguises. The most commonly recognized disguise is displacement, but identification is an equally important one. In displacement the patient narrates these attitudes in relation to a third party. In identification the patient attributes to himself attitudes he believes the analyst has toward him. Lipton (1977b) has recently described this form of disguised allusion to the transference with illuminating illustrations.

The analyst who believes it is necessary to be inactive lest he contaminate the transference waits for the transference to become clear spontaneously. Such a view overlooks the central fact of resistance. If resistance will gradually disappear if one but waits, why is interpretation necessary?

Stone's (1973) remarks are apposite here. He notes that, to his knowledge, Freud never changed his belief that "resistances are operative in every step of the analytic work." Yet many analysts seem to think that somehow, without interruption or interpretation, the patient's free associations in themselves will eventually reveal "the whole and meaningful story of his neurosis" in explicit terms. As Stone points out, "This is, of course, manifestly at variance with Freud's basic assumptions about the role of resistance, and the germane roles of defense and conflict in the origin of illness" (p. 49).

How much initiative the analyst will take in making transference interpretations depends on how ubiquitous he believes transference implications are in the patient's associations, how important he believes it is for these implications to become explicit, and how confident he is that they will spontaneously become explicit if he waits for this. Freud clearly advocates a good deal of initiative in making interpretations in general and interpretations of the transference in particular. While the following remarks quoted from Freud could be interpreted to refer to the analyst's silent reflection as well as to what he says to the patient, I believe they still reveal Freud's insistence on the analyst's initiative in offering explanations to the patient.

In *The Question of Lay Analysis* (1926b), for instance, Freud tells his interlocutor that one must "work over many tons of ore which may contain but little of the valuable material you are in search of." When the interlocutor asks him how one works over this raw material, Freud replies: "By assuming that the patient's remarks and associations are only distortions of what you are looking for—allusions, as it were, from which you have to guess what is hidden behind them. In a word, this material, whether it consists of memories, associations or dreams, has first to be *interpreted*" (p. 219). Similarly, Freud explains that the route to the patient's conflicts is indicated "by his symptoms, dreams and free associations. These must, however, first be interpreted—translated—for, under the influence of the psychology of the id, they have assumed forms of expression that are strange to our comprehension" (p. 205).

As to the transference in particular, Freud explicitly states: "The transference is made conscious to the patient by the analyst" (1925, p. 43). In *The Question of Lay Analysis*, he writes: "Analytic love is not manifested in every case as clearly and blatantly as I have tried to depict it. Why not? We can soon see. In proportion as the purely sensual and the hostile sides of his love try to show themselves, the patient's opposition to them is aroused. He struggles against them and tries to repress them before our very eyes. . . . He is also repeating before our eyes his old defensive actions" (1926b, p. 226). It is clear, then, that without the analyst's initiative in interpretation, these ideas will not become explicit.

Analysts by and large seem to favor a stance quite different from Freud's behavior as an analyst. Although, as Wisdom (1967) expresses it, most analysts adopt Freud's overall technique, clinical premises, and basic theory, they generally do not adhere to his style of scientific "testing." According to Wisdom, Freud appears to have taken initiative in trying to work out the puzzle presented in his patient's communications. Instead of simply waiting for the patient to reveal the solution, "he seems to have made endless conjectures in an attempt to find explanations, and then sought to apply these and test them" (p. 335).

If the analysis of the transference requires interpretation, any more or less general reluctance to interpret will clearly militate against the analysis of the transference. On the other hand, an analyst may show initiative in one kind of interpretation and not another.

Glover (1955) is insistently clear on the initiative the analyst must take in interpreting the transference and even claims that it is precisely such interpretation which plays an important role in bringing about the transference neurosis. He notes that one should not expect transference interpretations automatically to "loosen the analytic situation, bringing a flood of memories," or directly to effect the resolution of the transference. "*On the contrary, the transference-neurosis in the first instance feeds on transference-interpretation;* in other words, the transference, starting in a fragmentary form, tends to *build itself* on the foundations of transference-interpretation" (p. 130). Glover sees the analyst as risking failure if he simply assumes that the transference neurosis, without assistance, will eventually reveal itself to the patient in a way that carries conviction. "The real essence of the transference-neurosis," he explains, "can be extracted only as a result of laborious attention on our part" (p. 113). What is necessary is to *"uncover"* the transference neurosis — "it does not dance attendance on the analytic rule" (p. 136). Most emphatically, he states his opinion that *"faint-heartedness in making transference-interpretations is responsible for more stagnation in analysis than any other attitude"* (p. 177). Fenichel (1938–1939) has also remarked on the negative effects of failing to make "sufficiently definite transference interpretations" (p. 46).

Glover's advocacy of the analyst's taking initiative may also be seen in his comments on the occasional appropriateness of making transference interpretations very early in a *session*. In particular, he advises that in cases in which "the transference situation is over-congested," instead of waiting for a long string of the patient's associations, it may well be better to begin with transference interpretation of some remark made right at the start of the session. He does, however, caution the analyst not to "make a habit of this, or indeed of any other policy in analysis," for the patient soon catches hold of the idea and may even start "casting associative bait at the beginning of each session" (1955, p. 177).

The question of how much an analyst should tell a patient of what he believes he sees in the patient's associations is a complex one. To tell all is to throw tact to the winds, if not to engage in wild analysis. To withhold is subject to the danger of manipulating the transference. One rationale for withholding may be an unwitting adherence to a theory of abreaction, namely, that one should wait to make transference interpretations until the "tension" connected with the transference attitudes has built up to the point at which they become spontaneously expressed. Alexander (1935) has expressed a similar point of view with regard to the withholding of interpretations of content: "Those who consider emotional abreaction as the most important therapeutic factor will emphasize all those devices that may produce emotional eruptions resembling the abreactions in cathartic hypnosis: certain manipulations of the resistance, or the creation of emotional tensions in the patient, for example by avoiding interpretation of content" (p. 590). Fenichel (1938–1939) has written of "traumatophilic" analysts. Clearly no hard and fast rules can be given; but one must remember that countertransference can be rationalized easily in terms of a theory of therapy. In any case, any predetermined general policy, whether of initiative or restraint, is suspect.

Inactivity must not be confused with neutrality. Neutrality does not mean an avoidance of doing anything, but rather giving equal attention to all the patient's productions, without prior weighting of one kind of material over another, and confining oneself to the analytic task, that is, abstaining from deliberate suggestion. I have elsewhere (1979) described neutrality as including persistent attention to the inadvertent effects of the therapeutic setting and the therapist's interventions on the patient's experience of the relationship.

Stone (1954) describes well the manner in which one hopes the patient will perceive the analyst's neutrality. At an optimal level, he conjectures, the patient should feel "the analyst's neutrality [as] a self-imposed purposive technical discipline (in fact, a technique), willingly accepted for good reasons, neither employed as a personal gratification, nor rigidly embraced in panicky fear of rule breaking" (p. 575). If the analyst is alert to how the patient believes he is feeling, as I suggested above he should be, he will commonly find that the patient interprets the analyst's restraint as his "going by the book" for fear of violating the rules of analysis.

The analyst's waiting for things to become clear also reveals the misconception that one should not make an interpretation until one knows it to be true. Often one can be quite sure that, in the light of explicit references to the transference, certain nontransference material has *some* transference meaning, but one cannot be sure of what that meaning is. One cannot know whether an interpretation is correct until it has been made and tested against the patient's response. Otherwise it can only be a more or less plausible hypothesis. Wisdom (1967), for instance, writes that the analyst must look to what the patient says and does *"after* the interpretation." It is these responses from the patient that allow the analyst to determine whether or not his interpretation is correct. As Wisdom puts it, "the practical position is that clinical interpretations are established or not by their consequences" (pp. 335–336). Wisdom notes here that Kubie makes the same point in his "Problems and Techniques of Psychoanalytic Validation and Progress" (1952).

One of the objections to a heavy emphasis on the transference that one hears from both analysts and patients is that it means the analyst is disregarding the importance of what goes on in the patient's real life. This criticism is not justified. To emphasize the transference meaning is not to deny or belittle other meanings but to focus on the one of the several meanings of the content that is the most important for the analytic process. The analyst works on the premise that, of the many things to which the patient could associate, his choice is often dictated by a topic which can serve as resistance to the transference and it is therefore the transference implication that matters for the process.

Let us say a man associates about an angry outburst against his wife. The latent meaning for the analytic situation may be that he is angry about something the analyst has said but is unable to say so directly. An interpretation to that effect does not mean that the "real" meaning of his talking about the angry outburst against his wife is that he is angry at the analyst. It does not necessarily mean that he was unjustified in being angry at his wife, nor for that matter that he is unjustified in being angry at the analyst. What it does mean is that he has a resistance to expressing his anger openly to the analyst and that the matter of his outburst against his wife appears now in his associations as a disguised way of alluding to his anger at the analyst. The patient's associations, like symptoms and manifest dreams, are compromise formations between a wish and a resistance. In this instance, we see a compromise between the patient's wish to express anger against the analyst and whatever restraint is preventing him from doing so openly.

It is likely that an interpretation in the analytic situation about a trivial matter in the patient's real life is likely to be met with less resistance than the interpretation of an important matter. In the example above, an interpretation that the patient is alluding to anger at the analyst would have to be related to some plausible events of the analytic situation, as I shall later describe. Such an interpretation might be met by the rejoinder that it is his *wife* the patient is talking about, *not* the analyst. The interchange would proceed from there of course, not excluding the possibility that the analyst is mistaken, but also ensuring that the patient does not take the interpretation as a denial of the validity of his feelings about his wife in their own right.

Lipton (1977b) has pointed out that the patient's response may be influenced not only by the external importance of the matter or by whether the transference interpretation is unwelcome, but also by the implication the analyst's way of wording the interpretation has for him. The patient may feel the analyst is belittling the external reality if the analyst says: "What you really mean..." The latent content is not what the patient *really* means. The patient really means the manifest content. What the analyst has discerned is that a reason for the patient's dwelling on the subject in his associations lies in its latent meaning for the analytic transference. To say so is very different from saying what the patient "really means."

Another unfortunate form in which the analyst's interpretation may be couched is: "What you are saying is..." The latent content is not what the patient is saying. In fact the latent content is what the patient is *not* saying. The analyst therefore might better use the phrasing: "What you are not saying is. . ." But even this form of putting it has its dangers, for it can readily be understood by the patient to be a criticism. It seems to assert that the patient *ought* to be saying what he is not saying rather than what he *is* saying.

Perhaps the most neutral way for the analyst to make his point is to speak in the same sense in which I am discussing the transference content. The analyst might say, "A possible hidden meaning of what you are saying insofar as you and I are concerned is. . . ," or "An implication of what you are saying for our relationship is. . ."

The patient has to learn that the crucial technique of analysis is to find just this latent meaning. In time the patient is more likely to accept such an interpretation, even if it seems to deflect attention from some immediate life situation that is very important to him. At the same time, as with so many other issues in analysis, one must take care not to mistake the patient's compliance for genuine understanding and acceptance.

The issue is the basic one for technique of the connection between the analysis of the transference and the patient's real life situation. Patients have to learn that analysis is not designed to give them immediate and direct help with their reality situation but to help them understand themselves. This understanding helps them as they carry it over into their life situation. It may come as a great relief to patients to discover that the analyst is not going to try to tell them how they should live their lives. Gray (1973) has described well how the patient may find the analyst's restraint in discussing the patient's life situation as a reassurance of his neutrality. At first, however, if transference interpretations are made at a time when the patient is concerned about a particular real life situation, the patient may feel that this amounts to the analyst's ignoring the patient's real problems and being overly concerned with himself. Even after the patient has apparently learned that this is not so, the same objection may arise again as a new reality situation appears.

The patient may also misunderstand a transference interpretation of his associations about an external event to mean that the analyst is implying that the external event took place *because* of its meaning for the transference. If the patient describes an angry scene with his wife and the analyst interprets the latent meaning of these associations to be that the patient is angry at the analyst, the patient may mistakenly conclude that the analyst means he had the fight with his wife as a displacement of the fight he wanted to have with the analyst.

It is of course possible that to a greater or lesser degree the patient does carry out some action in the external world as a displacement of the transference, that is, that the patient is "acting out." An interpretation that this is the case, however, needs to be sharply distinguished from an interpretation of the meaning of the patient's associations for the transference. An interpretation of associations means only that the patient *tells* the episode at a particular point as a disguised reference to a latent meaning for the transference, while an interpretation of acting out is a conclusion that the behavior was *engaged in* as a way of expressing something about the transference. The patient's resistance may, of course, be so strong that he will omit to tell the episode during the hour. In that case one can only go by what one can infer from the manifest associations he does offer.

The issue of whether an action represents an acting out of the transference or merely appears in the associations as an allusion to the transference is often not clear-cut. The patient is likely to be more resistive, the more the interpretation proposes that the action was *undertaken* for transference reasons. Since the multiple determination of behavior makes it hazardous in any case to weight the relative importance of coexisting determinants, it is important to take up the issue of the relative roles of displaced action or merely indirect communication openly for joint consideration by the patient and the analyst. If a female patient starts an affair, who is to say what role is played by an acting out of the transference and what by her loneliness and fortuitous (of course the question is how fortuitous) meeting of an appropriate (or seductive) man? External reality is one of the determinants of behavior.

The relatively little-used concept "acting in" refers to a transitional phenomenon between acting out and telling, in that transference does not remain in the psychic sphere but appears as an action in relation to the analyst in the hour itself (see Zeligs, 1957). This was Freud's original use of the concept "acting out." It is in relation to such "acting in" that, as I mentioned above (p. 49), Freud (1914) says one counts it as a triumph if the impulse is remembered instead of being discharged in action. But I would argue that the first step is to make the impulse explicit in the here-and-now. Interpretations of allusions to the transference, then, are not only interpretations of allusions in the content of the patient's associations but also interpretations of the meanings for the transference of the patient's actions within, as well as outside, the analytic session.

In summary, the expansion of the transference in the analytic situation often demands a good deal of initiative on the analyst's part in interpreting allusions to the transference in associations not manifestly about the therapeutic relationship, as well as in the patient's behavior. There are important resistances to unmasking the disguised transference on the part of both the patient and the analyst. The analyst cannot know whether a conclusion he has formed about a transference is correct until he has proposed it to the patient and observed the patient's response, with attention not merely to the explicit response but to its possible implications too. Emphasis on transference meanings implies no belittling of the simultaneous other meanings in the patient's life but only that what is primarily important for the purposes of the treatment is the meaning in the transference.

5

THE UBIQUITY OF
TRANSFERENCE MEANINGS

TRANSFERENCES AND THE TRANSFERENCE NEUROSIS

Though analysts generally agree that the analysis of the transference is the heart of the process, the question of how pervasively the patient's productions have a meaning in the transference which is resisted is not often explicitly addressed.[1] One's view on how pervasive such meanings are will inevitably influence one's view on the role the interpretation of such meanings should play in the analytic process.

The question of the pervasiveness of implications for the transference in the patient's associations is closely linked with the question of the distinction between transferences and the transference neurosis. While it is commonly agreed that when there is a transference neurosis the transference plays an important, if not ubiquitous, role in the patient's associations, there is no consensus on when one can say a transference neurosis has developed. Before discussing the distinction between transference and transference neurosis, however, I shall review what various writers have said about how pervasive implications for the transference are in the patient's associations.

That Freud does not sharply state or emphasize his views on this issue is borne out by the difficulty I encountered in trying to find his comments on this issue. There is no direct statement in the papers on technique. In "The Dynamics of Transference"

---

[1] In the literature I cite below, the authors often speak of transference when they mean transference resistance. As I have pointed out, this confusion arises because the facilitating transference is often not recognized as a transference, so the distinction between the two kinds of transference is not made.

69

(1912a), however, one can reach a conclusion by deduction. I have already quoted Freud's remark that if something in the material of the neurotic complex "is suitable for being transferred" onto the analyst, then "that transference is carried out; it produces the next association, and announces itself by indications of a resistance" (1912a, p. 103). In the preceding paragraph, he explains: "The resistance accompanies the treatment step by step. Every single association, every act of the person under treatment must reckon with a resistance and represents a compromise between the forces that are striving towards recovery and the opposing ones" (p. 103). But even this juxtaposition does not necessarily lead to the conclusion that all associations have a reference to the transference, for Freud himself has listed other resistances than transference resistance (though I questioned this proposition earlier). Furthermore, Freud here implies that some subject matter might not be suitable to be transferred.

One quotation which is referred to on occasion as suggesting that he does indeed regard all the patient's productions as having a reference to the transference, whether explicit or implicit, is from his autobiography (1925). He declares: "We shall be justified in assuming that nothing will occur to him that has not some reference to that [the psychoanalytic] situation" (pp. 40–41). Yet even in this statement the question remains of what he means by the analytic situation.

The point can be clarified by a more direct but little-noted passage in The Interpretation of Dreams (1900). Freud writes that when the patient is told to say whatever comes into his mind, his associations become directed by "the purposive ideas inherent in the treatment," and that there are two such inherent purposive themes, one relating to the illness and the other—concerning which Freud says the patient has "no suspicion"—relating to the analyst (pp. 531–532). This statement could be read as meaning that the associations are directed sometimes by the illness and sometimes by the transference, but I believe that it means they are both present throughout.

On the other hand, there is another statement by Freud (1912a) which suggests that he does not believe that all associations have a meaning, whether explicit or implicit, for the transference — at least not at first. He claims: "The longer an analytic treatment lasts and the more clearly the patient realizes that distortions of the pathogenic material cannot by themselves offer any protection against its being uncovered, the more consistently does he make use of the one sort of distortion which obviously affords him the greatest advantages — distortion through transference. These circumstances tend towards a situation in which finally every conflict has to be fought out in the sphere of transference" (p. 104).

Two years later in "Remembering, Repeating and Working-Through," he again implies a process which grows in ubiquity insofar as the transference is concerned. As I have already noted (pp. 48–49), Freud indicates that given the patient's acceptance of the basic rules of the analysis, then all his symptoms will begin to acquire "a new transference meaning" and "his ordinary neurosis" will be replaced by a "transference-neurosis" which is to be worked through in the treatment (1914, p. 154).

A later statement in the *Introductory Lectures* (1916–1917) makes even clearer the progressive domination of the analysis by the transference. There, after pointing out that a neurosis is not static but continues to grow and develop, Freud defines a transference neurosis as that situation in which the "treatment has obtained mastery over the patient" (p. 444). He goes on to assert that the neurotic material now becomes focused on the relation to the analyst and claims that work with the patient's memories assumes a lesser role in the face of this heightening of the transference (see above, p. 45). Perhaps we can conclude that, for Freud, transference neurosis defines that stage of an analysis in which transference resistance becomes the preferred and principal means of distortion.

But if Freud's writings do not discuss more explicitly the issue of how ubiquitous transference implications are in the patient's associations, do other analytic writings on technique do so? In general, as I shall later elaborate, it is primarily the Kleinians who do stress this point. Nevertheless, the question is occasionally addressed by non-Kleinians. Bird (1972), for instance, writes: "It is also my belief that transference, in one form or another, is always present, active, and significant in the analytic situation. From this it should follow that rarely is there need to give up on the transference meaning" (p. 267).

A meticulous search of the analytic literature would probably turn up additional instances of explicit opinions on the ubiquity of transference meanings. Here, for example, is one from Wisdom (1956) which clearly states that such meanings are ubiquitous: "A train of contiguous associations (however unconnected they may seem to ordinary modes of thought) (a) have a meaningful inter-relation, and (b) in particular have a fundamental reference to the analyst" (p. 147). But Wisdom is a Kleinian, and I shall postpone the discussion of the Kleinian view of transference.

Various other examples can be found. Ferenczi (1925), admittedly following Otto Rank's suggestions, takes the patient's relation to the analyst "as the cardinal point of the analytic material" and sees "*every* dream, *every* gesture, *every* parapraxis, *every* aggravation or improvement in the condition of the patient as above all an expression of transference and resistance" (p. 225). Ferenczi here notes the precedent set by Georg Groddeck, who, if his patient's symptoms grew worse, would typically ask: "What have you against me, what have I done to you?" According to Ferenczi, Groddeck claimed that in the process of answering this question the patient's immediate symptoms abated and Groddeck himself came to a deeper understanding of the neurosis (p. 225).

More recently, McLaughlin (1975) points out: "As part of our work ego we have learned to 'read' the patient's ideational affective-kinesic content, no matter where centered, as having some level of relevance to his relationship to us, and we allow ourselves to resonate in this context" (p. 366). Similarly, Lichtenberg and Slap (1977) argue that within the analytic situation the analyst is always "listening" to how the analysand is experiencing him (the analyst). In other words, no matter what the apparent focus of the patient's remarks or even silences is, "one or (usually) more aspects of the patient's sense of himself interacting with his environment invariably has relevance to his relation with the analyst" (p. 299). Here one might also cite Nathaniel Ross's (1978) comment that the analyst must repeatedly direct attention to "the patient's affective relationship to him, no matter how displaced or repressed" (p. 11).

One of the most emphatic statements that all associations have a transference meaning is to be found in a book by David Shave entitled *The Therapeutic Listener* (1974). But I cannot follow Shave in his insistence that oral conflicts are the root of all psychopathology, nor in his idiosyncratic and surprising conclusion for technique of a general opposition to interpreting the transference.

Despite the fact that one can find statements that attest to the ubiquitous presence of transference resistance, this view is not generally stated as an explicit principle. On the contrary, the widespread acceptance of a distinction between transferences and transference neurosis frequently implies that only after the transference neurosis develops do transference resistances become ubiquitous. Now, a distinction can be made between transference as the patient's habitual way of relating to people in general, including the analyst, and the transference neurosis, which refers to attitudes that become manifest only after the analysis has been in progress for a time and seem to be more specific to the analyst. I would argue, however, that transference resistances, even if not signaling a transference neurosis, are present all the time. Whatever one's conclusion on whether they *should* always be interpreted, my point is that they are always present and hence potentially always interpretable.

Greenson (1967) offers a definition of the transference neurosis which conforms to the way it is often conceptualized. He notes: "Freud also used the term *transference neurosis* to describe that constellation of transference reaction in which the analyst and the analysis have become the center of the patient's emotional life and the patient's neurotic conflicts are relived in the analytic situation" (p. 34). Greenson cites as a reference the passage I quoted above (p. 49) about the "new transference meaning" all the patient's symptoms acquire (Freud, 1914, p. 154). One might also note again Freud's remark that the transference neurosis is in evidence when the "treatment has obtained mastery over the patient" (1916–1917, p. 444). But it is important to distinguish between the significance of the analyst in the hour and in the rest of the patient's life. It is noteworthy that an analysis can proceed quite well, with a clear-cut transference neurosis, even though many aspects of the patient's life are not talked about and find no role in the analysis. This omission does not necessarily mean that the patient is avoiding these matters. As I emphasized earlier, the associations which the patient brings are those which are suitable for expressing the transference resistances (in a disguised way) and the omitted data may simply not be suitable or necessary for this purpose. As is apparent from resistance to the resolution of transference, it is also true that explicit preoccupation with the transference during the hour does not necessarily bespeak a successfully progressing analysis.

So far as I know it is Glover (1955) who deals most explicitly and articulately with the distinction between transferences and the transference neurosis. He calls the transferences other than the transference neurosis the "floating," "working," or, most often, "spontaneous" transferences. He also clarifies that these transferences are the kind present before the transference neurosis develops.

Glover proposes a qualitative difference between transferences and the transference neurosis. Whereas the spontaneous transferences are the same as those which govern the person's current object relations, the transference neurosis comprises those transferences which repeat the processes of symptom formation and the infantile neurosis. In particular, he singles out the repetition of identifications in the transference neurosis and the way in which this reveals "the nature and progress of the most important infantile object relations" (p. 121). The transference neurosis, according to Glover, allows the analyst to confirm or revise his earlier impressions of these object relations. *"The transference-identifications occurring during the transference-neurosis enable the analyst to single out those phases of ego-development at which pathogenic fixations occurred"* (p. 122).

Glover cites the example of a mildly depressed patient. In the early part of the analysis this patient contended that his mother had "grossly neglected" him and it was his father who had provided a kind of maternal care. And, Glover notes, the initial course of the analysis tended to confirm this position. Once the transference neurosis became established, however, a negative father transference came to the fore. The "persistent analysis of the transference situation" unveiled an underlying "homosexual trauma": when the patient's sister was born, the father had seemingly switched his love to her. Glover comments: "This transference work was followed by a sharp improvement in symptoms and permitted the inference that his operative pathogenic fixation was to his father and that his super-ego introjection of the father was a highly ambivalent one" (p. 122).

Glover points to "this selective repetition" as distinguishing between the later-developing transference neurosis and the early spontaneous transference. In describing the spontaneous transferences as "working transferences," he explains that "they represent the potential attachments or aversions which govern the person's current object relations." Although he notes that in character disorders these early transferences may already take on a pathological form, it is the transference neurosis that, he believes, "brings to the fore transferences which have a specific connection with the processes of symptom-formation" (p. 122).

That Glover considers the patient's associations to have pervasive implications for the transference after the transference neurosis sets in is clear. Once the transference neurosis begins to develop, he writes, *everything that takes place during the analytic session, every thought, action, gesture, every reference to external thought and action, every inhibition of thought or action, relates to the transference-situation"* (p. 119). He adds that a transference interpretation may then be appropriate at any point.

Again, in the context of a discussion of countertransference and counterresistance, Glover underlines the pervasiveness of transference (and countertransference) phenomena. Some, he himself admits, might protest his insistence on the possible countertransference implications of the analyst's every action (or lack of action). Yet, he argues, "if analysts maintain, as they do maintain, that during the transference-neurosis everything the patient thinks, says or does can, if necessary or expedient, be interpreted as transference, then surely everything the analyst thinks, says or does during the counter-transference can, where necessary or expedient, be self-interpreted as counter-resistance" (p. 98). What is highlighted here is the overriding impact of the transference situation once the transference neurosis has developed.

It would be an error, however, automatically to read Glover

as saying that transference becomes ubiquitous only after the transference neurosis develops. He does say that the character of the transference changes. The working transferences have the same character as current object relations, while the transference of the transference neurosis relates to symptom formation and the infantile neurosis. The former are spontaneous while the latter develop only after regression through the analytic process.

Fenichel (1938–1939) does not distinguish explicitly between transferences and transference neurosis as Glover does. But he does contrast a generalized, rigid character attitude that is not specific to the analytic situation to "a 'transference situation' in the narrower sense in which the patient reacts to the analyst in a mobile and specific manner, in the same way as at one time in the past he reacted or wished to react to a certain definite person" (p. 67).

Loewald's (1971) distinction between transferences and the transference neurosis is similar to Fenichel's. He describes the transference as "essentially automatic responses, signs and symptoms of the old illness." The transference neurosis, on the other hand, is depicted as "a creation of the analytic work done by analyst and patient, in which the old illness loses its autonomous and automatic character and becomes reactivated and comprehensible as a live responsive process and, as such, changing and changeable" (p. 62).

The question of whether the concept of transference is applicable outside the analytic situation turns on this same distinction between those attitudes to the analyst which are the same as attitudes the patient has to other people and which are present from the beginning of an analysis and those attitudes which are specific to the analyst and develop in time only as a result of a regression brought about by the analytic situation. The matter is one of definition. Freud clearly includes displacements from the past to persons in the patient's life outside the treatment situation under his concept of transference. Nevertheless, the concept of transference has become so firmly connected to the therapeutic situation that term "extra-transference" does not mean "nontransference," but rather "outside the therapeutic situation." Extra-transference, then, may or may not be transference in the wider definition.

It is important to recognize that the patient's habitual ways of relating to people are not necessarily explicit in the patient's associations. The patient may be only peripherally aware of his suspiciousness, haughtiness, obsequiousness, or whatever. Glover calls these habitual attitudes "spontaneous" not because they are explicitly in awareness but because they appear spontaneously at the beginning of an analysis, in contrast to developing in specific relation to the analyst and the analytic process only as the treatment progresses. If the habitual attitudes are to be brought into awareness, they require interpretation just as the implicit attitudes of the transference neurosis do. Wilhelm Reich's (1933) "character analysis" refers to the interpretation of just such ego-syntonic attitudes. Indeed, his accomplishment was to show that they have to become ego-dystonic if the analysis is to progress into an interpersonal interaction specific to the analyst, that is, into a transference neurosis.

There remains considerable controversy among analysts over whether a transference neurosis is a necessary part of a successful analysis, as is attested by the wide divergence of opinion on the matter in a recent issue of the *Journal of the American Psychoanalytic Association* (see Blum, 1971; Calef, 1971; Harley, 1971; Loewald, 1971; Weinshel, 1971). This alone implies the central importance of the interpretation of transferences other than the transference neurosis.

Glover (1955) has taken the position that in many instances a transference neurosis does not develop despite the fact that the analysis may be successful therapeutically. Here he is not referring to cases in which ostensible success may be based on an unanalyzed transference. Rather, he points to neurotic patients who, while displaying both positive and negative spontaneous transferences, "are never caught up in the *transference-neurosis*" (p. 46). In Glover's opinion: "The view that a typical transference-neurosis develops in all the cases is not only theoretically improbable but contrary to actual experience" (p. 114).

Although he does admit the argument that the very prolongation of analysis without indications of a transference neurosis is itself a sign of transference neurosis, he believes this holds true only some of the time. Here he mentions those cases in which, despite the expense, the patient continues in an analysis that is quite obviously at a stalemate. According to Glover: "Only an ambivalent transference sufficiently strong to be regarded as a 'neurosis' can adequately account for this remarkable phenomenon" (p. 115). This somewhat obscure remark probably refers to a situation in which there is a transference primarily of defense which, even though not a transference neurosis in the ordinary sense of a repetition of the infantile neurosis, is sufficiently specific to the analyst and a result of the analytic situation that Glover chooses to call it a transference neurosis.

I suggest that either transference primarily of impulse or primarily of defense can serve as resistance to the development of a transference neurosis in that either can serve to defend against specific and regressive involvement with the analyst in a new version of the infantile neurosis. I mean that the analyst may be presented at the outset of an analysis either with an apparent absence of involvement with him or with florid transference wishes which are the same as those directed to outside figures and which defend against specific involvement with the analyst in the infantile conflict. Loewald (1971) describes such a case in which, although he had the data for a genetic transference interpretation, he recognized that what he could have dealt with as resistance to the resolution of transference was more appropriately dealt with as resistance to involvement in the tranference.

Loewald goes so far as to suggest that the transference neurosis can be silent:

> A decisive engagement, such as is represented by a fully developed transference neurosis, may never or not distinctly come to pass in an analysis. Yet the repercussions of what has occurred may turn out to be deeper and more far-reaching than anticipated... significant advances toward its resolution may go unnoticed by patient and analyst or may not be available for even disguised communication. The transference neurosis is by no means in all instances or at all times clearly visible and may even be largely a silent process without necessarily losing its impact. Some patients, throughout the analysis, maintain a distance from open emotional involvement with the analyst, and the analytic work may mostly take place at a considerable remove from the transference arena itself [1971, pp. 65–66].

I find Loewald's view unlikely. It differs from Glover's view that a transference neurosis may not develop, for Glover sees the therapeutic result in that instance as depending on work with the spontaneous transferences whereas Loewald refers to the analytic work taking place "at a considerable remove from the transference arena." While it might be, in some analyses, that a connection between the manifest transference and the past cannot be discerned, I would suspect that if there is no "open emotional involvement with the analyst," any effects obtained must be significantly based on an unresolved transference.

My consideration of the distinctions between transference and transference neurosis and between transference of wish and transference of defense enables me to state more clearly some of the issues of the ubiquity of transference. First, if it is conceded that the emergence of a transference neurosis means that transferences related to the infantile neurosis now find expression and *not* that it is only in the transference neurosis that transferences dominate the patient's associations, then it may be that transferences—albeit of the same kind that determine the patient's extra-transference relationships—are ubiquitous and dominate the patient's associations from the beginning on. Second, if it is recognized that not only transference of wish but also transference of defense is transference, then again it becomes more apparent that the formulation that transferences are ubiquitous and present from the beginning on is valid. A third consideration determining one's view on the ubiquity of transference is the extent to which one believes transference becomes enacted in behavior in the analytic situation. I have already discussed this issue in Chapter 3.

EARLY TRANSFERENCE INTERPRETATION

In opening my discussion on the ubiquity of transference meanings, I referred to my proposed distinction between transference that facilitates the analytic work—a true transference, mistakenly equated by some with an appropriately realistic attitude—and transference serving resistance. I said that the ubiquitous transference which can be interpreted advantageously is transference serving resistance.

Freud's (1913) oft-quoted warning against early transference interpretation does distinguish between facilitating transference and transference serving resistance. His formulation suggests that even if transference is ubiquitously present, it is not necessarily serving the resistance, and should be left untouched until it does so. He emphasizes: "*So long as the patient's communications and ideas run on without any obstruction, the theme of transference should be left untouched.* One must wait until the transference, which is the most delicate of all procedures, has become a resistance" (1913, p. 139).[2]

An even clearer statement of Freud's distinction is found in his *Introductory Lectures*:

> I must begin by making it clear that a transference is present in the patient from the beginning of the treatment and for a while is the most powerful motive in its advance. We see no trace of it and need not bother about it so long as it operates in favour of the joint work of analysis. If it then changes into a resistance, we must turn our attention to it and we recognize that it alters its relation to the treatment under two different and contrary conditions: firstly, if as an affectionate trend it has become so powerful, and betrays signs of its origin in a sexual need so clearly, that it inevitably provokes an internal opposition to itself, and, secondly, if it consists of hostile instead of affectionate impulses [1916–1917, p. 443].

The transference that "operates in favour of the joint work of analysis" and "should be left untouched" is the unobjectionable positive or facilitating transference while the transference that should be analyzed is the transference resistance. As we have already seen (pp. 14–15), Freud is quite definite in his contrast between facilitating transference and transference resistance. It is only after "a strong [positive] transference has been established" that the patient is able to use the analyst's communications (1913, p. 144). The positive transference provides the underpinning or "source of strength" which allows the work with transference resistance to proceed. It is in line with this that

---

[2] The translation is misleading. It should read: "One must wait with this most delicate of all procedures [dealing with the transference] until the transference has become a resistance."

Freud stresses reserving transference interpretation for what is transference resistance.

Freud does indicate that transference resistance can be present at the very beginning of an analysis, but the illustration he gives is so gross a resistance as silence. In our paper on the early analysis of transference, Muslin and I conclude that Freud bases his formula on a model of analysis in which a freely communicating patient is mistakenly considered to be free of transference resistance (Gill and Muslin, 1976). In contrast, we believe that "covert references to the transference, like resistance, in fact as transference resistance, are present every step of the way and, subject to the usual issues of judgment about when an interpretation should be made, should be interpreted when they appear, even if that be early in the analysis" (pp. 792–793). In other words, even in a patient who is talking freely, transference resistance will be present, in addition to the more obvious facilitating transference. Consistent with the usual principle that priority of interpretation goes to resistance, we argue that this transference resistance should be interpreted.

Stone (1973) makes the same point: "Only with time and increasing sophistication did it become evident that fluency, even vividness of associative content, indeed tendentious 'relevancy' itself could, like overcompliant acceptance of interpretations, conceal and implement resistances which were the more formidable because expressed in such 'good behavior' " (p. 46).

Here we might note that as early as 1923 Ferenczi and Rank wrote that a strong positive transference, especially near the beginning of analysis, is only a symptom of resistance which requires unmasking. This remark can be seen as a forerunner of Wilhelm Reich's (1933) attitude toward the early analysis of the transference. He, too, said that an early positive transference should be "unmasked."

Indeed, over the years a number of analysts have recommended that transference analysis be begun early. In 1946, for instance, Sylvia Payne described an advance in analytic technique which "aims at using transference interpretation at the earliest opportunity, utilizing a systematic employment of a transference interpretation whenever reference to a personal relationship takes place, the object being to set in operation the transference neurosis as quickly as possible" (p. 14). By "personal relationship," I believe Payne means an extra-transference relationship. In other words, she is saying that from the beginning the analyst interprets such extra-transference references as allusions to the transference.

More recently, Brenner (1969) has voiced decided objections to the formula that transference should never be analyzed early. He finds no basis either in practice or in theory for the insistence that only transference manifestations "clearly in the service of resistance" should be analyzed. "On the contrary," he argues, "transference should be dealt with and interpreted like anything else in the analytic material: that is, as it appears and in accordance with its importance at the moment relative to other material" (p. 337). Brenner explains the misguided precept as following from Freud's giving too great a role to the positive transference in overcoming initial resistance in contrast to the need to interpret resistance. Brenner's remark is not entirely clear, however, because one does not know what he means by saying that transference should be interpreted even if it is not "clearly in the service of resistance."

Stone's (1973) remarks may throw light on Brenner's meaning here. Stone suggests that the classical dictum be modified. Instead of saying that "one does not interpret the transference until it becomes a manifest resistance," one should stress that at this point interpretation becomes *obligatory* (p. 59). But even before this, Stone proposes, "resistance to awareness [of the transference] should be interpreted, and its content brought to awareness, as soon as the analyst believes that the libidinal or aggressive investment of the analyst's person is economically a sufficient reality to be influencing the dynamics of the analytic situation and/or the patient's everyday life situation" (p. 59). Muslin and I make a similar distinction between obligatory and optional interpretation (Gill and Muslin, 1976).

By a manifest resistance whose interpretation is obligatory, Stone presumably means a situation in which the transference resistance is explicit or in which, even if it is not being verbalized, it has brought about so gross a resistance as silence. The other kind of interpretation, which Stone suggests is desirable even though optional, is the same as what I, too, have called interpretation of resistance to the awareness of transference, or of indirect allusions to the transference (see Chapter 2).

Zetzel (1966-1969) also takes issue with the contention that early references to the analytic situation should be avoided. She is convinced "that serious problems in subsequent transference analysis may frequently be attributed to failure in the initial phases of treatment to achieve a secure therapeutic alliance by a suitable verbal intervention" (p. 205). As I shall indicate later, however, by "suitable verbal intervention," she does not necessarily mean transference interpretation.

The contemporary form of the injunction against early transference interpretation is in fact that one must wait until the "therapeutic alliance" has been established. This formulation is an indication, as I shall later discuss, that the concept of therapeutic alliance serves for what Freud called the unobjectionable positive transference. Rangell (1968) exemplifies this view. He describes how, at the beginning of an analysis, the patient tests the analyst to see how he will receive various kinds of disturbing information. Yet he does not believe that this early interaction entails "transference displacements or distortions" per se. Instead, he views it as an attempt by the patient "to establish the realistic position and characteristics of the analyst" (p. 21). Rangell goes on to suggest that only by fostering this "reality" base to begin with can the analyst proceed to effective interpretation of transference distortions. He elaborates in a footnote:

> One may argue that in a technical sense, transference appears at once even in the instances first noted, and that the testing described may already reveal an intrinsic suspiciousness displaced from unconscious infantile sources. However, it can be countered that the testiness may also be considered to be ego-adaptive behavior, appropriate to the situation of caution before a 'stranger' and not at all a displaced transference neurotic phenomenon. Of course both types of reaction can also occur together [p. 21n].

That "both types of reaction" do "occur together" rather than as a dichotomy is my position throughout this monograph, and I conceptualize this indistinguishable interweaving of transference and realistic attitudes as the transference elaboration of a real situation.

Of course an early tactless interpretation of transference will interfere with an alliance, just as Freud indicates one can forfeit the positive transference by injudiciously taking sides with someone with whom the patient is in conflict (1913, p. 140). But presumably any interpretation, not only an early interpretation, should take into account what the patient is able to hear usefully at the time. In her response to Zetzel's (1958) presentation on the therapeutic alliance in the psychoanalysis of hysteria, Grete Bibring remarks on her confusion by the paper, in that "the emphasis on the first few hours—of tact, handling and management of transference—obtains all through the analysis" (Leach, 1958, p. 565). One can only agree. What remains to be stressed is that while a tactless interpretation may interfere with the alliance, an early tactful interpretation of transference may be the best means of fostering an alliance and may even be essential to it.

I conclude, then, that Freud's precept against early transference interpretation resulted from his failure to recognize the manifestations of transference resistance in the apparently freely associating patient. I also agree with Brenner that Freud overemphasized the role of the positive transference in overcoming resistance as against the tactful interpretation of transference. I am suggesting that, optional rather than obligatory though it be, the early interpretation of transference is often desirable and that Freud's injunction against it should no longer be maintained. I believe his injunction also reflects his failure to give the analysis of the transference the central role I believe it should have. The fact that a distinction can be drawn between earlier transference resistances and a later transference neurosis does not militate against the principle of the primacy of transference interpretation throughout an analysis, including its beginnings.

6

THE CONNECTION OF ALL
TRANSFERENCE TO THE ACTUAL
ANALYTIC SITUATION

Various authors (e.g., Kohut, 1959; Loewald, 1960) have emphasized that Freud's early use of the term "transference" in *The Interpretation of Dreams* (1900, p. 562) reveals the fallacy of considering that transference can be expressed free of any connection to the present. In this early context, Freud uses "transference" to refer to the fact that an unconscious idea cannot be expressed as such, but only as it becomes connected to a preconscious or conscious content. In the phenomenon with which Freud is here concerned—the dream—transference takes place from an unconscious wish to a day residue. To extend this definition, we could say that just as the day residue is the point of attachment of the dream wish, so must there be an analytic-situation residue (though Freud does not use that term) as the point of attachment of the transference (using the term now in its present-day restricted definition). This parallel between dream day residue and transference analytic-situation residue has been noted by Schmideberg (1953), Kohut and Seitz (1963), Bordin (1974), and Bergmann and Hartman (1976).

The proportions in which the patient's experience of the relationship is determined by the past or the present vary widely and may change markedly from point to point in the analysis. But the idea of an attitude determined solely either by the past or by the present is an abstraction. This is true even for attitudes that are appropriately adapted to the interpersonal situation, for all behavior is built on the past as it is intrapsychically represented and the individual nuances of even apparently similar adaptive behaviors will reflect this past. On the other hand, since total estrangement from reality is well-nigh impossible, all behavior bears some relationship to a "stimulus" in the present, however idiosyncratically interpreted. Even a deteriorated schizophrenic will show some response to the current situation. No matter how inappropriate behavior is, it has some relation to the present, and no matter how appropriate it is, it has some relation to the past.

Analysts have always limited their behavior, both in variety and intensity, in order to increase the extent to which the patient's behavior is determined by his idiosyncratic interpretation of the analyst's behavior. Probably largely motivated by an attempt to keep the transference as free from any influence by their own behavior as possible, analysts have placed increasing restrictions on their activity, compared with Freud's practice.

But no matter how far the analyst attempts to carry this limitation of his behavior, the very existence of the analytic situation provides the patient with innumerable cues which inevitably become his rationale for his transference responses. In other words, the realistic situation cannot be made to disappear — the analytic situation *is* real. It is easy to forget this truism in one's zeal to diminish the role of the realistic situation in determining the patient's responses. Freud himself may have lost sight of it in one of the reasons he offers for using the couch: "I insist on this procedure [the couch], however, for its purpose and result are to prevent the transference from mingling with the patient's associations imperceptibly, to isolate the transference and to allow it to come forward in due course sharply defined as a resistance" (1913, p. 134). The transference cannot be kept from intertwining with the real situation, but Freud may here mean only that with fewer reality cues the transference may become easier to disentangle.

The argument that a transference interpretation intrudes the analyst as a reality into the analytic situation is a persistent remnant of the false precept that the analyst can indeed be only a reflecting mirror. An effort to deny the real impact of the analyst can only result in its remaining implicit so that it exerts its effects without being understood.

Bordin (1974) states the situation well: "There can be no absolutely blank screen. Even the most unrelentingly literal conformity to this specification cannot completely efface partial cues to the person of the analyst. The patient, usually starved for cues to the analyst's personality, notes his taste in decor, his books and periodicals, his ways of walking and talking, his inflections, the timing of rustling sounds, connoting shifts in body position, and, of course, his physical appearance" (p. 13).

If the analyst remains under the illusion that the reality cues he provides to the patient can be reduced to the vanishing point, he may be led into a kind of silent withdrawal. This picture is not too distant from the caricature of the analyst as someone who indeed refuses to have any personal relationship with the patient. (Here I am using the term "personal relationship" in Lipton's [1977a] sense, to distinguish it from the analyst's technical interventions.)

Lipton (1977a) has suggested that the unresponsive analyst may be responsible for making the patient appear more narcissistic than he is, because the patient has not really been given the opportunity for an object relationship. Namnum (1976) takes a similar view. He insists: "A transference can only develop in the climate of a human and to some degree reciprocal relationship" (p. 111). In his opinion, Freud did not intend to prohibit any "spontaneous participation" on the analyst's side. In fact, Namnum contends, the attempt at complete anonymity or total abstinence may even interfere with the analysis of transference. A good "working relationship is promoted by the analytic work itself, performed with genuine personal interest which does not conflict with neutrality" (p. 115).

In further clarifying the issue of responsiveness, Lipton (1977a) distinguishes between the listening analyst and the silent analyst. The latter sees his silence as a technical device. He is silent not merely because he is listening but because he means by his silence to convey some specific message, such as that he finds the patient's associations too trivial or too repetitive to respond to — however obscure this intention may be to the patient. Of course the listening analyst may be misconstrued by the patient as a silent analyst.

Glover (1955) is clear on the dangers of a general policy of silence with a silent patient: "To meet the silence invariably with silence is to court a sort of silent combat, which confirms the obstinate or aggressive type of patient in his view that analysis is a kind of psychological pugilistic encounter to be settled by the gaining of points" (p. 99). In fact, Glover points out, one needs specifically to confront this type of patient with the negative transference implications in his attempt to make the analysis a contest of wills.

It is difficult to know how many analysts actually do conform to the stereotype of the silent, passive analytic stance. There are fashions in analytic styles too. The analyst of today may be surprised to read Glover's impression in 1955 that "nowadays analysts are much less disposed to listen in the same continuous receptive way as formerly: and that, on one pretext or another. . . make more frequent or copious interpretations even in the early stages of analysis" (p. 96).

The attitudes a patient develops toward a silent analyst are not entirely transference, nor are they free of any influence from the present. An analysis of the patient's reaction will reveal that the analyst's silence is the current stimulus to which the patient responds with more or less plausible attitudes determined by a past experience. These attitudes may range from regarding the silent analyst as benevolent and omniscient, to seeing him as sadistically withholding. These are not uncontaminated transference attitudes, but include an effort to cope with the reality of the silence. An understanding of the situation requires not only making these transference attitudes explicit but also recognizing that the patient considers the analyst's own silence to be a plausible explanation for them.

Brockbank's (1970) excellent criticism of excessive silence deserves to be quoted. He calls the conclusions the patient draws from the analyst's silence "inadvertent interpretations," and suggests that silence can subvert neutrality rather than promote it. In addition to "inadvertent interpretations," he sees such prolonged analytic silence as intensifying the patient's "hypnotic readiness." Here Brockbank refers to the heightened impact of any communication from the analyst:

> The silent analyst sets the stage for an analysis in which suggestion plays a highly important role. In these instances, the patient tends to give the analyst the kind of materials the analyst wants in the manner in which he wants it because of the unavoidable element

of suggestion inherent in every interpretation. . . . The patient is, in fact, placed in a state of hypersuggestibility not unlike that of the hypnotic situation because of the analyst's silence. As a result, the patient is ready for any hint or clue which he can use in order to be fed, loved or appreciated by the analyst. In this way excessive silence may become a contamination which may destroy analytic neutrality [p. 459].

He describes an interesting case of a patient who, when he was most circumstantial, repetitive, and perseverative, and when the analyst was most silent, went away feeling that he had an unusually good analytic hour. Brockbank understands this as the patient's having avoided the pain and stress of a real relationship with the analyst.

One may ask how much silence is "excessive" silence. Clearly the answer cannot be a quantitative one; rather, it lies in the purpose of the silence. If, as Lipton (1977a) puts it, the silence is being used as a technique to influence the patient and is not simply because the analyst is listening, it is excessive silence. Of course precipitate interpretation of tiny hints from the patient is also behavior by the therapist which plays a role in the patient's attitudes. Once again—the analyst cannot do nothing.[1]

The Limitation on the Analytic Situation as Research

A variant of the idea that the transference can be expressed without "contamination" is the confusion between analysis as research and research on the data of the analytic situation. Ever since Freud said that in the conduct of an analysis research and therapy are combined, analysts have continued to believe that

[1] An interesting variant on this theme of the inevitability of the analyst's participation can be found in Macalpine's (1950) argument against regarding the transference as arising spontaneously from the patient. She considers the transference to be an adaptation by regression to the infantile setting of the analytic situation. Her contribution may have been obscured because she limits her discussion of the therapeutic setting to those aspects which she conceives of as forcing the analysand into a regression to an infantile state. Moreover, instead of emphasizing, as I do, the fact that *whatever* the analyst does plays a role in determining the transference, she defines the analyst's behavior only in terms of the analytic situation and neglects the interpersonal aspects.

their reports of their analytic experience constitute research. It should be remembered that Freud also said that evidence "in support of the correctness of our hypotheses is obscured in our treatment" and should be sought elsewhere, for "a therapeutic procedure cannot be carried out in the same way as a theoretical investigation" (1910b, p. 142).

While it is foolish to insist that only certain kinds of activity deserve to be called research, it is important to distinguish between an analyst's reporting of his cases and systematic research on the data of the analytic transaction.[2] The latter requires the establishment of hypotheses beforehand, some method of collecting the data so they are reproducible, ratings by independent judges where clinical variables are involved, and the assessment of results by the rules of logic, which may or may not take a statistical form.

Influenced to some extent by the model of research in the natural sciences, and considering that the only kind of research possible in the analytic situation is that conducted by the practicing analyst on his own cases, analysts attempt to keep the field uncontaminated by their interventions. In describing the "essentially research and nondirective attitude of the analyst," Greenacre (1954) writes: "It is therefore just as necessary to keep the field pure for the clear reflection of the memories emerging from the past as it is to avoid contaminating the field of surgical operation or to avoid getting extraneous dirt onto a microscopic slide" (p. 681).

The analogy to research in the physical sciences leads to the conclusion that the patient's material should be produced without having been influenced by the analyst. This reasoning strengthens whatever other forces motivate the analyst to keep his interventions to a minimum. Once again the fallacy in this reasoning is that the existence of the analytic situation itself constitutes an unavoidable interaction. Loewald (1970) has persuasively discussed the difference between the role of the researcher as a detached observer in the natural sciences and the analyst as a participant in the analytic situation.

The feeling persists among analysts that the interpersonal in-

---

[2] I owe the clarification of this distinction to discussions with Hartvig Dahl.

teraction is an unfortunate interference and complication. To emphasize it in either theory in general or the theory of technique in particular arouses uneasiness and a fear that an interpersonal point of view will overshadow and crowd out the unique contribution of psychoanalysis to intrapsychic psychology. Interpersonal and intrapsychic are somehow considered antagonists. Only such an attitude, it seems to me, would account for a view like that of Rangell (1968), who rejects the idea that identification with the analyst plays any role in the analytic process and says that the patient identifies only with the analytic *functions* of the analyst (p. 25).

A remark made by Anna Freud (1954) over 25 years ago still seems to me to capture the feelings of many psychoanalysts today. She refers to Stone's distinction between "real personal relationship" in the analytic situation and "true transference reactions." According to her, many analysts indicate that the transference, the patient's "fantasied relationship to the analyst," dominates the treatment from the beginning; only at the end does the real relationship emerge. In contrast, she believes that, at least in most neurotic cases, the reverse holds true:

> We see the patient enter into analysis with a reality attitude to the analyst; then the transference gains momentum until it reaches its peak in the full-blown transference neurosis which has to be worked off analytically until the figure of the analyst emerges again, reduced to its true status. But — and this seems important to me — to the extent to which the patient has a healthy part of his personality, his real relationship to the analyst is never wholly submerged. With due respect for the necessary strictest handling and interpretation of the transference, I still feel that somewhere we should leave room for the realization that analyst and patient are also two real people, of equal adult status, in a real personal relationship to each other. I wonder whether our — at times complete — neglect of this side of the matter is not responsible for some of the hostile reactions which we get from our patients and which we are apt to ascribe only to "true transference." But these are technically subversive thoughts and ought to be "handled with care" [p. 373].

Why "subversive"? What is the danger involved in recognizing the real relationship, that it must be "handled with care"? How does this recognition interfere with the "necessary strictest handling and interpretation of the transference"? Might its recognition not prove to be a necessary part of such strict handling and interpretation of the transference?

The issue of the relationship between the intrapsychic and the interpersonal has wider implications for psychoanalytic theory than in the analysis of the transference. Psychoanalysis is often considered to overemphasize the intrapsychic determinants of behavior in relation to the interpersonal determinants. In his book on psychoanalytic psychotherapy and behavior therapy, Wachtel (1977) has written clearly on the distinction between the intrapsychic and interpersonal models. It is true that psychoanalytic theory does include both models, but it tends to stress the intrapsychic. A genuinely integrated view would recognize that behavior is a resultant of both kinds of determinants. The individual sees the world not only as his intrapsychic patterns dictate, but also as he veridically assesses it. Furthermore, the two kinds of determinants mutually influence each other. The intrapsychic patterns not only determine selective attention to those aspects of the external world which conform to them, but the individual behaves in such a way as to enhance the likelihood that the responses he meets will indeed confirm the views with which he sets out. This external validation in turn is necessary for the maintenance of those patterns. It is this last insight that psychoanalytic theory often ignores, postulating instead an internal pressure to maintain the intrapsychic patterns without significant reference to the external world. One of the attractions of Piaget's theories is that his formulation of the twin processes of assimilation and accommodation is an integration of the two models. External input is assimilated to existing schemata, but these also accommodate to the input (cf. Wachtel, 1980).

The unique contribution of psychoanalysis is the demonstration of the power and persistence of the intrapsychic determinants. But these determinants become only artificial abstractions if they are dealt with in isolation from the interpersonal context in which they find expression.

The Absence of an Agreed-Upon Term for the Actual Analytic Situation

Because Freud tends to take the realistic aspects of the analytic situation for granted and alludes to them only in passing, there is no agreed-upon term for these realistic aspects. It would seem obvious that what Freud (1913) calls "rapport" must have significant determinants in the actual situation. Yet that Freud (1925, p. 42) can write that the transference develops "without the physician's agency" indicates his deemphasis of the analyst's real behavior toward the patient—in effect taking for granted that this behavior is appropriate. He thus sets a model for continuing deemphasis of the analyst's actual behavior in the theory of analytic technique.

I believe that an important reason for Freud's taking an appropriately realistic attitude on the analyst's part for granted and failing to focus explicitly on the characteristics of the actual situation is that he does not regard these appropriately realistic attitudes as agents of change or recommend their deliberate employment to produce change. On the contrary, he explicitly sees the change resulting from the positive transference as merely suggestion; it is not what he considers specifically analytic: "Often enough the transference is able to remove the symptoms of the disease by itself, but only for a while—only for as long as it itself lasts. In this case the treatment is a treatment by suggestion, and not a psycho-analysis at all" (1913, p. 143). What Freud does make explicit, however, is the *deviation* from the taken-for-granted appropriate attitudes on the analyst's part, namely, the countertransference.

To regard the unobjectionable positive transference as no more than the patient's realistic attitude to the analyst is sharply inconsistent with the great stress Freud lays on the positive transference as an affective factor in opening the patient to influence. It ignores the pains he takes to argue that even though the positive transference, that is, suggestibility, plays this important role in the analytic process, analysis differs from other suggestive treatments in that the transference is analyzed (1916–1917, pp. 450–453). And indeed such a view overlooks the significance of Freud's calling these attitudes transference in the first place.

That by the positive transference Freud does not simply mean the realistic relationship becomes clear in this passage from "Analysis Terminable and Interminable": ". . . not every good relation between an analyst and his subject during and after analysis was to be regarded as a transference; there were also friendly relations which were based on reality and which proved to be viable" (1937a, p. 222). Later in the same paper, he reaffirms his early definition of the positive transference as "the affectionate attitude... which is the strongest motive for the patient's taking a share in the joint work of analysis" (p. 237).

Analysts have largely followed Freud in taking it for granted that the analyst's behavior is such that the patient's appropriate reaction to it·will be cooperation in the joint work. But there are significant interactions between the patient and the analyst which are not transference but to which the patient's appropriate response would not be cooperation. If the analyst has given the patient cause to be angry, for example, and the patient is angry, at least some aspect of the anger is neither transference nor cooperation — unless the idea of cooperation is confusingly stretched to mean that any forthright appropriate reaction of the patient is cooperative since it is a necessary element in continuing an open and honest relationship. We do conceptualize inappropriate behavior on the analyst's part as countertransference, but what is our name for an analysand's realistic response to countertransference?

In considering the analysand's realistic responses, it might be well to distinguish between their affective and cognitive aspects. I have already suggested that it is incorrect to regard the unobjectionable positive transference as simply or even primarily realistic, even though it may be consonant with what would be realistic affective attitudes, granted appropriate behavior on the analyst's part. But the concept of the unobjectionable positive transference also fails to connote the currently determined cognitive aspects of the patient's realistic attitudes. Though Freud clearly regards the affective factor in the patient's attitudes to the analyst as the more important one, he does allude to a cognitive factor in terms of the patient's intellectual interest and understanding. In the paper on technique of 1913, after discussing the role of the positive transference, he points to "yet another helpful factor": "the patient's intellectual interest and understanding." But he adds that "it is always in danger of losing its value, as a result of the clouding of judgement that arises from the resistances" (p. 143).

I believe that even though they can be separated only conceptually, we should distinguish realistic and transference aspects of the analytic relationship. Because the positive transference, consonant though it is with the present (assuming appropriate behavior on the analyst's part), is primarily affective and so heavily rooted in the past, I believe we should continue to call it the positive — as against the erotic — transference. The cognitive attitudes appropriate to the actual analytic situation should then be called "realistic."

Although, until recently, the concept of the realistic relationship has played little role in analytic discussions as an explicitly focused-on term and concept, it has been mentioned from time to time, more or less in passing. Freud uses the term "actual situation" in his autobiography (1925, p. 42). But he more often uses the term "real" for the actual situation. In "The Dynamics of Transference" (1912a), for instance, he notes that if the father image is the determining one in the positive transference, "the outcome will tally with the real relations of the subject to his doctor" (p. 100). And he mentions how, in the face of transference resistances, the patient "is flung out of his real relation to the doctor" (p. 107). A page later he describes the patient's attempt "to put his passions into action without taking any account of the real situation" (p. 108). In his summary of technique in "An Outline of Psycho-Analysis," Freud (1940) writes of how "The analytic physician and the patient's weakened ego [base] themselves on the real external world" (p. 173).

Brief references to the realistic relationship can be found throughout the literature. Alexander, French, et al. (1946), for instance, remark that not all the patient's reactions to the analyst are transference reactions; some are appropriate to the therapist's actual personality characteristics and behavior (p. 72). Similarly, Stone (1973) notes in passing that "the patient's ego reacts to the analyst always, to a varying degree, in terms of the perceived and immediate realities" (p. 57).

Greenson specifically focuses on this issue in his article "The 'Real' Relationship between the Patient and the Psychoanalyst" (1971). Here he uses the word "real" to mean both genuine and realistic. Because even unrealistic aspects of the patient-analyst relationship are after all genuine, it would be better to use the term "realistic" than "real." Greenson and Wexler (1969) have also introduced the term "nontransference" to cover all relations in the analytic situation other than the transference. Because "nontransference" defines something negatively, I again prefer the positive designation "realistic."

In speaking of the realistic relationship, I do not mean to imply some standard of absolute external reality. In particular, I do not mean to imply such a reality, of which the analyst is the arbiter. I mean, rather, a consensually validated concept of the actual situation arrived at by discussion and "negotiation" between the two participants in the analytic situation.

The Alliance

A growing feeling that Freud's writings on transference fail to take adequate account, at least explicitly, of the distinction between transference and the realistic relationship is responsible for the more recent introduction of concepts of various kinds of "alliance." There is precedent in Freud, however, for the term "alliance." He writes that "the analytic situation consists in our allying ourselves with the ego of the person under treatment, in order to subdue portions of his id which are uncontrolled — that is to say, to include them in the synthesis of his ego" (1937a, p. 235). Here it is clear that the idea of an *alliance* is not restricted to the attitudes of the patient but refers to a relationship with implications for both participants. We ally ourselves with the patient's ego.

Yet I shall argue that the various alliance concepts suffer from the same failure to distinguish clearly between present and past determinants of the patient's attitudes as does the concept of the unobjectionable positive transference. The alliance concepts simply emphasize the present and cognitive determinants, whereas the unobjectionable positive transference emphasizes the past and affective determinants. In taking realistically appropriate behavior on the analyst's part for granted, both deemphasize any examination of the actual situation.

Zetzel (1958) defines the "therapeutic alliance" as a "real object relationship which fosters mobilization of autonomous ego attributes" (p. 186). She finds forerunners of the concept in the writings of Edward Bibring and Richard Sterba. In his contribution to the symposium on the theory of the therapeutic results of psychoanalysis, Bibring (1937) sees the analyst's attitude and the "atmosphere" he sets up as providing a kind of "reality-correction" for the patient. He underlines his belief that "the patient's relationship to the analyst from which a sense of security emanates is not only a precondition of the [analytic] procedure but also effects an immediate. . . consolidation of his sense of security" (p. 183). According to Bibring, this "immediate consolidation," while not a result of the analytic work per se, must in some sense be "coordinated" with the treatment if it is to be of value. Sterba, in his frequently quoted paper "The Fate of the Ego in Analytic Therapy" (1934), stresses the patient's identification with the analyst in his realistic analyzing functioning. It will be noted that Bibring's vantage point is primarily the analyst while Sterba's is the patient. They both, however, emphasize realistic attitudes.

One would think, therefore, that by therapeutic alliance Zetzel means primarily the current realistic relationship; yet she also finds determinants of the alliance in the past. In fact Zetzel makes the same distinction Freud made between transference that serves the purpose of resistance and transference that does not, so that her concept of therapeutic alliance seems the equivalent of Freud's concept of the unobjectionable positive transference. For Freud's transference facilitation versus transference resistance, she counterposes transference and transference neurosis. She notes, for instance: "A differentiation is made between transference as therapeutic alliance and the transference neurosis, which, on the whole, is considered a manifestation of resistance" (1956, p. 170).[3] In summarizing her position, however, Zetzel indicates that "as transference analysis impinges on

[3] Tartakoff (1956) makes the same distinction between facilitating and obstructing transference in a review of de Forest's book *The Leaven of Love* (1954). She claims that de Forest fails to distinguish "between those transference manifestations which permit a working relationship in analysis based on the patient's trust and confidence in his analyst and the transference-neurosis" (p. 333).

the basic conflicts . . . transference neurosis and therapeutic alliance tend to merge to a degree which may make them indistinguishable" (1958, p. 195). Her formulation is similar to Freud's postulation of a transition from facilitating transference to transference resistance, but Freud's description has the advantage of keeping the two concepts separate.

Greenson (1965) has coined the term "working alliance." He prefers this term to "therapeutic alliance" because it "has the advantage of stressing the vital elements: the patient's capacity to work purposefully in the treatment situation" (p. 157). For him, too, the working alliance includes both realistic and transference aspects. He admits, for instance, that "the working alliance may contain elements of the infantile neurosis which eventually will require analysis" (p. 158). Thus, even though he differentiates the transference neurosis and the working alliance as entailing "essentially different transference reactions" (p. 156), he, like Zetzel, tends to blur the distinction between facilitating transference and transference resistance. It also becomes clear that his designation of the "real relationship" (1971) encompasses the realistic relation as a whole, not simply the realistic aspect of the working alliance. In delineating this real relationship, he is "emphasizing object relations including and beyond the scope of the concept of the therapeutic or working alliance" (p. 214).

Sandler, Dare, and Holder (1973), like Zetzel, add "autonomous functions" to the idea of the unobjectionable positive transference to arrive at their proposal of a "treatment alliance." Their concept of the treatment alliance, like the concepts of therapeutic and working alliances, includes the realistic and the transferential. They point to Freud's (1913) distinction between the patient's establishing "a friendly rapport and attachment" to the analyst and the obstructing transference. In their opinion, Freud's use of "the term 'transference' for both these aspects of the relationship has been a source of confusion in subsequent literature and has contributed to the persisting use of the term 'positive transference' to designate aspects of what we refer to here as the treatment alliance" (pp. 28–29). Part of what these authors, like Loewenstein (1969) and Hendrick (1939), want to distinguish is rapport and transference, but they, too, mistakenly believe that

Freud's "unobjectionable positive transference" refers primarily to the current realistic aspects of the relationship. As I have argued, Freud himself regarded the positive transference as primarily based in the past.

Kanzer and Blum (1967) read Freud as I have. They write: "The distinction within the 'positive transference' of an element, which is actually the realistic therapeutic alliance, should clarify a source of theoretical and practical confusion" (p. 109). That the positive transference to which they refer is Freud's unobjectionable positive transference becomes clear in their reference to "the healthy aspects of integrated transference dispositions," their distinction between the transference neurosis and the transference, and their description of the transference as "entrenched at the genetic and functional core of the personality" (p. 109). In the latter phrase especially it becomes clear that they mean the same thing Freud meant in defining transference as the capacity for human relatedness, the basis of influenceability. The "theoretical and practical confusion" they mention is that exemplified by Sandler et al. (1973), who misunderstand why Freud defined the friendly rapport as a transference.

The absence of any agreed-upon definition of the various alliances may be seen in how various authors sometimes consider them to be the same, sometimes see them as different, and sometimes depict one as an aspect of another. Dickes (1975), for example, regards the working alliance as the realistic aspect of the therapeutic alliance.

Friedman (1969) discusses the relative roles of realistic and transferential attitudes in the therapeutic alliance. He asks whether the alliance *can* be based on relatively autonomous aspects of ego functioning, or whether, rather, it must depend on attitudes toward the analyst which are more appropriately designated transference. His reasoning helps one understand Freud's use of the term "transference" for both facilitating and obstructing displacements from the past. Friedman contrasts the usual formulation of the alliance in the spirit of Sterba's (1934) rational ego to Nunberg's (1928) emphasis on how the patient's basic aims are opposed to the analyst's. The choice, as he sees it, is "between a therapeutic alliance without a motor or an energetic alliance without an obvious therapeutic orientation" (p. 145). He emphasizes that some major driving force in the patient must be involved in the therapeutic alliance. The analyst, he concludes, must simultaneously accept the patient for what he is and ally himself with the patient's hope to become diffferent.

Friedman misstates Sterba's position somewhat. As a matter of fact, Sterba does acknowledge the role of the positive transference in enabling the patient to assess the transference resistance rationally. He explains: "Through the explanation of the transference situation that he receives the. . . subject's consciousness shifts from the center of affective experience to that of intellectual contemplation. . . . In order that this new standpoint may be effectually reached, there must be a certain amount of positive transference, on the basis of which a transitory strengthening of the ego takes place through identification with the analyst" (1934, p. 365).

I have suggested that Freud failed to highlight and name the realistic aspects of the analyst's behavior because he wished to avoid the suggestion that these behaviors should be deliberately engaged in as agents of change. I believe this view is borne out by critics of the alliance concepts, who indicate that these concepts do imply that various analyst behaviors should be deliberately undertaken as technical measures to foster and promote an alliance and that this occurs at the expense of analyzing the transference.

Kanzer (1975), for one, considers that the therapeutic alliance and working alliance, as defined by Zetzel and Greenson respectively, are at opposite ends of a "continuum defined by the analytic pact, and show a marked tendency to depart from the guidance offered the traditional analysis by the fundamental rule" (p. 48). He concludes that the behaviors on the therapist's part that both Zetzel and Greenson propose for the development of the alliance belong to psychoanalytically oriented psychotherapy rather than to psychoanalysis. Specifically, he believes that Zetzel neglects the transference in favor of reassurance and Greenson neglects the transference in favor of a focus on the real situation. On the other hand, Kanzer does point out that "realistic and nontransference aspects of the patient-physician relationship. . . are all too often submerged in one-sided considerations of the transference" (p. 60). He agrees that these realistic aspects are not adequately conceptualized in traditional technique and that some theoretical formulation is needed to deal with them.

Curtis (1979) has criticized the alliance concept on the same grounds as Kanzer. He, too, believes that emphasis on the collaborative aspects of the analytic relationship is part of a tendency to "extend our sphere of interest beyond the patient's intrapsychic life to embrace all aspects of the therapeutic relationship" (p. 159). He fears that this emphasis may lead to a corrective emotional experience and away from analyzing transference and resistance.

It is true that some illustrations by proponents of the therapeutic alliance do appear to advocate transference manipulation rather than analysis. Zetzel's (1958) illustration, for example, of how to deal with early manifestations of anxiety does appear to utilize reassurance rather than interpretation. She describes a patient who was anxious about entering analysis for fear that she would appear contemptible or ridiculous. The first few hours produced material revealing the patient's increasing tendency to view the generally silent analyst as "an unreal, omnipotent figure." When the situation was discussed in the candidate's supervisory session, he became aware of his rigidity and voiced his concern about doing anything that might be considered nonanalytic, especially as this was his first analytic patient. "He adopted subsequently a slightly more active and human attitude, indicating to the patient his recognition of her anxiety. As a result the patient reported the next day that until yesterday she had thought of the analyst as a distant, Olympian, somewhat magical figure" (p. 190). To adopt deliberately "a slightly more active and human attitude" is to manipulate the transference. Even the recognition of the patient's anxiety, if carried out for the purpose of reassurance, as seems the case here, is a manipulation. In contrast, transference interpretation would mean pointing out that the patient had apparently concluded that the analyst was unreal and omnipotent on the basis of his not saying anything or some other aspect of his demeanor. It might well be that such an interpretation would lead the patient to find him more "human." Indeed, the patient said she realized that her picture of the analyst had been fantastic and that he was after all an ordinary man. But she reached this conclusion not through the insight engendered by a transference interpretation but via a transference manipulation.[4]

The alliance concepts have certainly elicited strong and contrasting reactions from analysts. On the one side, these concepts appear to have arisen in response to a belief that the realistic aspects of the analytic situation were being ignored. On the other side, some analysts see them as promoting a manipulation of the transference at the expense of analyzing it. Those who emphasize the distinction between transference and reality often do so with some implication of fighting for the rights of the downtrodden patient. They imply that analysts who see their patients' attitudes as entirely or primarily transference arrogantly consider their own attitudes to be invariably correct. These critics appear to believe that the analyst is often haughty and remote and that the patient suffers from not being regarded as a fellow human being. Their writings sometimes sound like a plea for analysts to be humane and to grant patients some degree of interaction. Whether or not analysts who emphasize the distinction do indeed intend such a slant, they are often considered to be urging this.

Analysts who downplay the distinction, on the other hand, often seem to regard those who focus on it as betraying a softhearted inability to maintain an appropriate neutrality in the face of patients' demands or importunities—as retreating from transference analysis to psychotherapeutic interaction. Rangell (1969), for example, insists that the alliance should not be used to assuage infantile needs, which need, instead, to be analyzed. In his opinion, "It is the analyst's objective and analysing function which is the 'real' relationship between patient and analyst" (p. 72). Here Rangell specifically objects to Greenson's (1966) notion of a kind of maternal concern and Gitelson's (1962) analogy to parental support in response to the child's dependent situation. It is precisely these kinds of distortions of the patient-analyst relationship, Rangell argues, that must be seen in terms

---

[4] After this was originally written, Brenner's (1979) criticism of Zetzel's case report appeared. (It is based on a fuller description of what is apparently the same case [Zetzel, 1966].) Brenner's point of contention is essentially the same as mine.

of the transference neurosis. "The pull towards a nurturing type of alliance based on early object ties," he continues, ". . . usually leads to a reliance on interpersonal gratification rather than on the imparting of insight, or, as Arlow and Brenner (1966) have pointed out, on ' "acting human" rather than—interpretation', and in practice often stimulates as well as obscures counter-transference reactions" (p. 73).

Rangell does not see the analyst's "scientific" perspective as "anti-humanistic." In his words: "An objective and scientific attitude can, and indeed should, go hand-in-hand with analytic empathy, caring, and compassion, a combination sensitively pointed out by Leo Stone (1961), without needing to invoke any contradictory or mutually exclusive attitudes on the part of the analyst" (pp. 72–73).

Though Rangell speaks approvingly of Stone, Kanzer (1963) has criticized Stone on the same grounds on which Rangell takes issue with Greenson and Gitelson. Stone (1961) argues that "primitive transferences. . . will tend to be superfluously activated or intensified, as the 'mature' ego syntonic transference requirement is inadequately gratified" (p. 106). Kanzer counters that, as he interprets Stone, such matters as Stone's telling his patient in certain instances where he is going on his vacation, his recommendation that the terminal phase include several sitting-up sessions in which the patient and the analyst get to know each other, as well as the general tenor of his discussions of the relation between science and humanity, may betray a failure to analyze the transference properly. Yet, whatever Stone's practice, I agree with what I understand his intention to be—a return to a base line of the analytic situation which resembles Freud's picture. The contrast here is to the withdrawn analyst who promotes what is in fact not a reinstatement of the past but an undesirable iatrogenic regression.

Lipton (1977a) has recently dealt with the same issue in a useful way. He describes a strong tendency in current practice, in contrast to Freud's, to obliterate the distinction between the analyst's technical and nontechnical behavior and to regard all the analyst's behavior as determined by technical considerations. His discussion is in the context of an examination of Freud's (1909b) analysis of the Rat Man. How should we characterize Freud's giving the Rat Man a meal, sending him a postcard, asking for a picture of his fiancée? Some analysts might, of course, consider such behaviors countertransference. The point is that there is a broad range of behaviors in which analysts personally differ widely from one another and which may or may not be countertransference. The crucial distinction is between those who believe that all of the analyst's behavior should be part of technique, is therefore subject to technical principles, and should be deliberately engaged in with technical intent, and those who believe that there is inevitably a nontechnical side to the analyst's behavior, which differs from analyst to analyst according to his personal predilections, and that this aspect is spontaneous and without therapeutic intent.

While Lipton's position is related to the idea of a taken-for-granted human or humane aspect of the analyst's behavior, it has the merit of explicitly distinguishing this aspect of behavior from technique. Aside from the fact that it is impossible in principle to eliminate the personal variable in a therapist's behavior, if only because therapists differ as persons, the effort to subsume the entire relationship under technique has undesirable consequences for the therapy situation. One of these is that it robs the personal relationship of the spontaneity it must have to be genuine. Stone (1954) contends that "a *complete* merging of the analyst as an individual and the analyst as technician may also be inimical to the analytic process" (p. 575). He suggests that the personal and technical sides of the analyst may afford a kind of "psychodynamic balance" with the patient's experiencing and observing egos. "Is it not rational to assume," he asks, that "a grave imbalance on one side may seriously affect the other?" (p. 575).

Glover (1955) approaches this distinction between the analyst's personal and technical behavior by remarking, in regard to "fringe-contacts": "when in doubt behave naturally." He cautions, however, that "a routine once established cannot be broken without provoking immediate transference reactions" (p. 24). Similarly, he advises: "Once the patient is off the couch the situation existing between patient and analyst is governed by everyday rules of politeness and consideration" (p. 44). He goes on to speak of certain situations in which behavior off the couch should become a subject of interpretation, but he warns against

overdoing this. Since the patient already sees the analytic relationship as quite one-sided, "unless the interests of the analysis
positively demand it, there is no need to rub this in" (p. 44).

It must be emphasized that the analyst's technical and personal behaviors are both real and that the patient responds in
transferential *and* realistic ways to both. In particular, the analyst's personal behavior may well have unintended repercussions on the transference which must be analyzed.

As we have already seen, Rangell (1969) exemplifies this
blurring of the technical and nontechnical aspects of the analyst's
behavior, as well as the failure to recognize that they are both
real, in his remark that "It is the analyst's objective and analysing function which is the 'real' relationship between patient and
analyst" (p. 72). The "analysing function" is technical and only
part of the real relation. Nor do "analytic empathy, caring, and
compassion" comprise the totality of the real relation.

The various alliance terms connote essentially what Freud intended to connote by the "unobjectionable positive transference."
But they, too, fail to make sufficiently explicit several further
distinctions that are needed: (1) With the patient, we need to
differentiate between the affective attitude directed toward reality — the positive transference — and the cognitive factors directed toward reality, which do not have the same interpersonally determined roots in the past. (2) With the analyst, we need
to distinguish between his technical and personal behaviors.

For some analysts, the alliance concepts at least have the virtue of naming the compound of the patient's realistic and transferential attitudes, which must always be assessed in judging
whether the patient can profit from a particular interpretation.
For others, however, the concept of an alliance carries the implication that the realistic relation must be deliberately fostered
as a matter of technique, at the expense of the analysis of the
transference. That implication is not a necessary one. The realistic relation is present whether the analyst wills it or not.

The analyst's behavior, like the patient's, can be divided into
realistic and (counter)transference reactions. Both his technical
and personal behaviors comprise varying mixtures of realistic
and countertransferential attitudes. Like the patient's positive
transference, the analyst's positive countertransference has an

unobjectionable and an erotic side. But, as with the distinctions in the patient's behavior, the distinctions in the analyst's behavior can be isolated only conceptually. In any actual instance, they occur in varying combinations.

Much of the criticism of Freud's technique stems from his unabashed personal relationship with his patients. Important though the recognition of the distinction between the technical and personal roles of the analyst is, I believe the current tendency to dissolve this distinction completely is a sign of a more basic problem—the failure to recognize the importance of the analyst's real behavior and the patient's realistic attitudes and how they must be taken into account in technique. It is to these technical issues I now turn.

7

THE ACTUAL ANALYTIC SITUATION
IN ANALYSIS OF TRANSFERENCE

In the preceding chapter I argued that no matter how much the analyst may limit the range and intensity of his behavior the analytic situation remains an interpersonal one, albeit one in which the patient's information about the analyst's attitudes is restricted. I shall now argue that the primary implication of this for the analysis of transference is that the patient's attitudes from the past become as plausibly related to and justified in terms of this restricted information about the analyst as the patient can make them.

All analysts would doubtless agree that there are both interpersonal and intrapsychic determinants of the patient's attitudes, and probably no analyst would argue that a patient's attitude can be formed without contamination, as it were — that is, without some connection to something interpersonal in the analytic situation. Nevertheless, I believe the implications of this fact for technique are often neglected in practice. There is a great difference between a general acknowledgment of the role of the analyst as a real person and the moment-to-moment taking into account of the real relationship between the patient and the analyst by interpreting how it appears to the patient.

Anna Freud (1954) has described how the analyst is a participant in a relationship by noting the nuances of difference in an analyst's real behavior with different patients:

> Just as "no two analysts would ever give precisely the same interpretations," we find on closer examination that no two of a given analyst's patients are ever handled by him in precisely the same manner. With some patients we remain deadly serious. With others, humor, or even jokes, may play a part. With some the terms

in which interpretations are couched have to be literal ones; others find it easier to accept the same content when given in the form of similes and analogies. There are differences in the ways in which we receive and send off patients, and in the degree to which we permit a real relationship to the patient to coexist with the transferred, fantasied one [pp. 359–360].

According to her, these slight differences in the analyst's responses can serve as clues to the patient's healthy personality — to his ego maturity, his intellectual capacities, and his ability to see his conflicts objectively at times. Unfortunately, she views these minute instances of "acting out" in the analyst's technical behavior only as leading to an understanding of the patient's character structure. She fails to recognize that these subtle bits of *reality* may be points of departure for the patient's transference elaborations.

The reality of the analytic situation plays a vital role in both aspects of the analysis of the transference — resistance to the awareness of transference and resistance to the resolution of transference. I shall first take up resistance to the awareness of transference.

Presented with such a narrow range of cues, the patient develops as plausible a hypothesis as he can to account for his experience of the relationship on the basis of this restricted information. The analyst will be alert to the way in which extra-transference material may allude to the transference if he remains mindful of the reality aspects of the analytic situation, both in terms of its context and his interventions. If he has announced he will miss a session, for instance, he must expect direct or indirect allusions to the patient's response. (In this regard, Lipton [personal communication] has suggested that the common view that the patient's reaction is primarily to the impending absence rather than to the manner of the announcement is mistaken.) If he makes an interpretation which he realizes the patient may take as a criticism, he should be prepared to interpret ensuing associations about unduly critical people as an allusion to the transference.

It is not only that the analyst will be more likely to recognize allusions to the transference if he keeps the reality of the analytic situation in mind. He will also be able to make his interpretation of such an allusion much more plausible and hence acceptable to the patient if he can point to the likely connection between this interpretation of an allusion to the transference and the reality which he suggests is its precipitant.

There are many variants of the patient's experience of the relationship in the analytic situation, both in terms of whether he feels the situation justifies his experience and in terms of how aware he is of the stimulus to which he is responding. His attitudes may range from a subjective sense of certainty that his experience is justified by the current situation to a felt conviction that it is not. He may believe he knows exactly what triggered his response, or he may have no idea what did. Of course the analyst must be alert to the explicit references the patient makes to his experience of the relationship, to features of the analytic situation, and to connections the patient draws between the two. It is characteristic of the analytic situation, however, that the patient is either only fleetingly aware of these matters or mentions them only casually in passing because they are the subject of resistance. A common sequence of associations is a glancing reference to the relationship followed by discussion of an extra-transference situation, which carries on the transference attitudes by allusion.

One might ask whether there is a contradiction between the view that the patient's transference attitudes are as plausibly related to cues in the actual situation as possible and the fact that these cues are often quickly disavowed and disappear from awareness. The reply is that resistance to the awareness of transference attitudes inevitably extends to the related cues as well. The disavowal of both cues and attitudes probably repeats the patient's disavowal of how he understood the earlier experiences which are the genetic basis of the transference attitude.

The analyst's views of what the patient is likely to respond to in the analytic situation may be quite different from what does indeed impinge on the patient. Analysts are often surprised by the patient's seeming obliviousness to what the analyst considers major features of the situation, but it is important to remember that this obliviousness may be only apparent. On the other hand, something the analyst feels is trivial may loom large to the patient.

This difference in the importance the patient and the analyst ascribe to an occurrence often leads to the typical situation in which something happens in the relationship which the patient seems to ignore. The analyst may respond by saying that the patient seems to be avoiding the topic and surely must have some thoughts about it. The analyst may be correct, but he may also be mistaken. It may be that the occurrence is of no importance to the patient or, even if it is, that the patient's response is a realistic one which he felt no need to say anything about.

Let us assume, however, that the analyst is correct in believing that the event did have some repercussions on the transference. If the analyst then complains that the patient is failing to report them, he himself may be failing to recognize that the associations the patient *is* giving may have as their latent theme a reference to the significance of the event which has taken place. (Of course even if the analyst does look for an allusion to the event in the patient's associations, he may be unable to see it, whether because of his inability to make the connection or because it is so obscured by the resistance.) Moreover, if the analyst complains that the patient is failing to give the proper associations, the patient will inevitably feel criticized. Since the fundamental rule is that the patient should tell whatever is in his mind, the analyst is in effect saying: "Although you are telling me what's in your mind, I'm not satisfied because there is something else that ought to be in your awareness." The analyst's intuitive recognition that the patient is resistant to talking explicitly about the transference has led to the analyst's dissatisfaction with the patient's associations and his complaint that the patient is not associating properly.

Glover (1955) deals with this issue by warning against conducting a fishing expedition for associations without some concrete idea in mind. He points out that in his experience, if he directs the patient's attention to some event "simply for the purpose of obtaining associations to that event," the patient typically reacts as if this were a criticism (p. 178). In addition, Glover notes, even if this response is analyzed, the event per se acquires significance. If this situation arises again, the patient will now deliberately act in a certain way, as if anticipating or provoking the analyst's response. We can draw a parallel here to our earlier discussion of dealing with acting out by an interdiction, instead of an interpretation of how the associations the patient does offer may be allusions to the event the analyst has in mind.

Lipton (1974) has pointed out that if a complaint that the patient is not free-associating is ever justified, it is so only if the evidence is clear that the patient is consciously withholding associations. So long as the patient continues to verbalize what is consciously in his mind, he *cannot* be guilty of failing to associate "properly" since his only instruction is to say "everything that is in your mind."

Another common error made by an analyst who is convinced of the importance of transference but maladroit in its interpretation is to interpret that the manifest content has an implicit transference meaning solely on the basis of a predicated parallel between the two, without making it plausible by reference to some feature of the analytic situation. Just as the patient attempts to find a realistic basis for his experience of the relationship, so must the analyst find as plausible a realistic basis as he can for his interpretations of this experience. In doing so, he underscores the importance of looking at what is actually going on.

If something has occurred in the analytic situation which the analyst feels must have affected the patient's experience of the relationship, but he is unable to see this in the patient's associations, he can always ask for the patient's assistance. He might, for instance, remark: "I suspect that what you are talking about may be in some way a continuation of what happened, but I'm unable to see the connection. Can you?" Similarly, if the patient's associations seem to hint strongly at a parallel experience in the analytic relationship, but the analyst cannot see what in the situation serves as a plausibly realistic basis for this reaction, he can again ask for the patient's help. He might say: "The theme of this hour is that you feel criticized by someone and I suspect you feel criticized by me, but I do not see what I have said or done that you might have taken as a criticism. Are you feeling criticized by me? And if so, what do you think has led you to feel that way?"

In discussing Strachey's (1934) paper on the therapeutic action of psychoanalysis, Rosenfeld (1972) also objects to mechanical transference interpretation. He mentions how some analysts at times reference all the patient's productions to the transference.

They automatically comment: " 'You feel this about me now' or 'You are doing this to me.' " Or they may simply "repeat the words of the patient parrot-like and relate them to the session." Rosenfeld argues that while such a "stereotyped" response masquerades as "an interpretation of the here-and-now situation, [it] changes Strachey's valuable contribution of the mutative transference into something absurd" (p. 457).

For the analyst to be alert to the reality aspects of the patient's attitudes, it is necessary that he see himself always as a participant in a relationship. Only if he considers himself a blank screen could he conceive of a patient's responses being dictated entirely from within the patient.

A consequence of the analyst's perspective on himself as a participant in a relationship is that he will devote attention not only to the patient's attitude toward the analyst but also to the patient's view of the analyst's attitudes toward the patient. The patient is likely to be more reluctant to voice, or even to be aware of, his speculations about the analyst's attitudes toward him than he is with his attitudes toward the analyst. Obviously, in general, a patient would feel that to speculate about the analyst's attitudes amounts to analyzing the analyst and attempting to turn the tables. The patient is especially likely not to mention attitudes toward him he believes the analyst would wish to disavow and which, to some degree, he is correct in believing the analyst holds. It is therefore all the more incumbent upon the analyst to be ready to offer his ideas on what he believes the patient may think he feels about the patient.

Though this differentiation between how the patient feels toward the analyst and how the patient feels the analyst feels toward him is not often explicitly stated, Glover does offer this remark in passing: "Obviously many of the functional resistances which we have been describing could also be called transference resistances in so far as the activity of any particular mechanism is expressed through the patient's reactions to the analyst or through the imagined reactions of the analyst to the patient" (1955, p. 67).

The analyst must remember that he may very well have been responsive to a greater or lesser degree to the patient's effort to repeat his past in the transference by behaving in ways which do indeed justify the patient's view of how the relationship is structured (Levenson, 1972). It is not to be wondered at that the analyst will unsuspectingly inevitably fall in with the patient's transference wishes to a greater or lesser degree for a longer or shorter time. To deny this is to deny that the analytic situation is indeed an interpersonal interaction. Sandler (1976a, 1976b) has recently discussed this issue under the labels of the patient's search for an "identity of perception" and the analyst's "role-responsiveness."

A question which inevitably arises from the emphasis on the necessity for the analyst to recognize his participation as a real figure is whether such recognition requires his agreeing or disagreeing with the patient's ideas about him. Greenson (1967, pp. 17–18), for example, describes a patient who, late in an analysis, was finally able to say that he found Greenson somewhat dogmatic and overtalkative. Greenson acknowledged the correctness of the patient's observation, but transference interpretation does not require such validation. In fact, that could deflect attention from an inquiry into the reasons for the patient's having delayed making what he considered to be a correct observation, and seems to have done so in Greenson's account.[1]

A confession places a burden on the patient since it implies a warding off of criticism. Confession seems appropriate only in the instance of a significant countertransference which the analyst judges continues to be an obstacle to the treatment because it has not been acknowledged. It is enough to deal with the patient's conjectures as meriting serious examination of their plausibility.

One must distinguish between validation of a perception and validation of an inference or judgment. Furthermore, one must distinguish between validation of the "truth" of an inference and validation of its plausibility. A good interpretation may well validate both a perception and the plausibility of an inference but take no position on its "truth."

An analyst's denial that he has the feelings a patient attributes to him is even less defensible than confession. Not only is it not

---

[1] Brenner (1979) has made the same point about Greenson's account in an article published after this was originally written.

persuasive in any case, but it may put the analyst in the unten-
able position of denying that he may be influenced by something of which he is unaware. As I suggested above, a posture of
certainty on the analyst's part is generally an unfortunate one.
What is desirable is, rather, as thorough an uncovering of the
patient's mental content as possible, including calling attention
to ideas the analyst believes the patient may have but is not stating.

Nor is it necessary for the analyst to take any position, as often seems to be implied in discussions of this sort, on how much
the patient's reaction is intrapsychically determined by the past
and how much it is determined by the actual interpersonal interaction. All that is necessary is a continuing elucidation of the
patient's view of the analytic situation as an integral part of the
analytic process. The analyst's position that he is dealing with
plausible hypotheses on the patient's part provides the appropriate atmosphere.

The careful examination of which features of the analytic situation lead to the patient's interpretations can play an additional and very important role in the difficult task of the analyst's becoming aware of his countertransference. For the search for
such features may bring to his attention aspects of his behavior
of which he was unaware.

The Resolution of Transference in the Here-and-Now

Earlier (p. 40) I quoted Freud's (1912a) direct reply to the
question of why transference is so eminently suited to serve resistance. His answer implies two steps in the interpretation of
transference. The first is to make the patient aware that "he
seeks to put his passions into action" (p. 108), that is, to interpret resistance to the awareness of the transference, and the second is "to compel him to fit these emotional impulses into the
nexus of the treatment and of his life-history," that is, to interpret resistance to the resolution of transference by making both
interpretations relating to the analytic situation and interpretations relating to the genetic past.

Strachey (1934) also proposes two steps in a "mutative" interpretation. In the first step "a portion of the patient's id-relation to the analyst is made conscious in virtue of the latter's position as an auxiliary super-ego" (p. 21). In my formulation this means that if the transference idea is not already conscious, the analyst makes it so by interpreting allusions to the transference in the explicit nontransference associations. The second step "depends upon his [the patient's] ability, at the critical moment of the emergence into consciousness of the released quantity of id-energy, to distinguish between his fantasy object and the real analyst" (p. 23). I have emphasized how this distinction is facilitated by interpreting the transference as a plausible explanation of something that has actually taken place between the patient and the analyst—the reality cues that are the patient's point of departure for his transference elaboration.

In sharply redirecting attention to the unique value of transference interpretations as compared with extra-transference interpretations, Strachey (1934) points to two major advantages of transference interpretations. One is that the interpretation is affectively immediate because it is about an impulse which is being felt and expressed toward the very person who is making the interpretation. The other is that the analytic situation is the most favorable setting for seeing that the patient's attitude does not necessarily stem from the actual situation, for in the analytic situation both participants have first-hand knowledge of the situation and an interest in being objective about it, which is not true in discussion of an extra-transference situation. As Strachey puts it: "in the case of an extra-transference interpretation the object of the id-impulse which is brought into consciousness is not the analyst and is not immediately present, ... and [because] the object of the id-impulse is not actually present, it is less easy for the patient. . . to become directly aware of the distinction between the real object and the phantasy object" (p. 34). He explains that the effectiveness of mutative interpretations may well "depend upon this fact that in the analytic situation the giver of the interpretation and the object of the id-impulse interpreted are one and the same person" (p. 36n).

Strachey indicates that his paper only elaborates on Freud's (1925) remark: "The transference is made conscious to the patient by the analyst, and it is resolved by convincing him that in his transference-attitude he is *re-experiencing* emotional relations which had their origin in his earliest object-attachments during the repressed period of his childhood" (p. 43). But Freud in fact stresses the role of the past in resolving the transference much more than Strachey does.

Thirty-three years after Strachey's paper, Stone (1967) makes the same points in recognizing the "unique effectiveness of transference interpretations." According to Stone, "No other interpretation is free, within reason, of the doubt introduced by not really knowing the 'other person's' participation in love, or quarrel, or criticism, or whatever the issue. And no other situation provides for the patient the combined sense of cognitive acquisition, with the experience of complete personal tolerance and acceptance, that is implicit in an interpretation made by an individual who is an object of the emotions, drives, or even defenses, which are active at the time" (p. 35).

I referred earlier to the fact that despite his emphasis on transference interpretations, Strachey notes, apparently with approval, that most interpretations are extra-transference interpretations. It may be that when Strachey refers to extra-transference interpretations, he means interpretations that are made in terms of relating the extra-transference material to the transference, but, if so, his account is misleading. For relating extra-transference material to the transference is designed to resolve the transference and is therefore a transference, not an extra-transference, interpretation.

I can usefully restate this distinction by referring to Rosenfeld's (1972) remarks on Strachey's paper. He believes that transference interpretations initiate "the mutative process," but a subsequent period of working through is needed to strengthen and further this process. Here Rosenfeld indicates that both transference interpretation and working through entail "not only the elaboration of the patient's fantasies and behavior in the transference but link[ing] the patient's conflicts in detail with his present life situation and his past" (p. 457). Rosenfeld also points out that "some analytic material seems at first sight quite unrelated to the transference and the analyst's interventions and interpretations must begin with an attempt at clarification" (p. 458).

What may not be recognized is that Rosenfeld is talking about three different steps in analytic work without sharply distinguishing them. The first is *clarification* of extra-transference material to get a clue to the allusion to the transference which lies in it. The second is bringing this transference into awareness, and the third is resolving the transference. "Elaboration of the patient's fantasies and behavior in the transference" probably refers both to interpretation of additional aspects of the transference not yet in awareness and to work toward resolving the transference within the analytic situation itself by comparing the transference and the features of the actual analytic situation from which it takes its point of departure. "Link[ing] the patient's conflicts"—presumably as expressed in the transference—to "his present life situation and his past" means resolving the transference by transference interpretations, on the one hand, and genetic transference interpretations, on the other.

For this careful comparison of the actual features of the analytic situation and the patient's interpretation of them, the features must be clearly delineated and focused on. It becomes clear then how a knowledge of these features is essential to the resolution of transference insofar as that resolution is dependent on work within the analytic situation.

The overcoming of resistance to the resolution of transference means that the patient must come to see that certain attitudes are indeed transference, or at least to recognize the role played in his attitudes by what he brings to the situation. This is often described as his coming to see how he is distorting the real situation, or how the real situation differs from what he conceives it to be. It would be more correct to say that the patient develops a hypothesis than that he distorts the actual situation. "Distortion" is an appropriate designation only for those instances in which the influence of the past contradicts the information in the present. If the analyst recognizes that the patient is attempting to be as rational as he can with what he has to work with, he is respecting the patient's sanity. If, on the contrary, he focuses on the patient's experience of the relationship without looking for something real that the patient may be responding to, he implies that the patient is manufacturing his experience out of whole cloth.

A more accurate formulation than "distortion" is that the real situation is subject to interpretations other than the one the patient has reached. The analyst suggests that the patient's conclusions are not unequivocally determined by the real situation. Indeed, seeing the issue in this way rather than as a "distortion" helps prevent the error of assuming some absolute external reality of which the "true" knowledge must be gained. The analyst need claim only that the situation is subject to various interpretations and that since the patient's conclusions are not unequivocally determined by the features of the situation which can be specified, he would be wise to investigate how his interpretation may in part be influenced by what he has brought to the situation. While it is in general not an unreasonable presumption that the analyst's view is more objective than the patient's, this may be untrue in a particular instance. In any case, the analyst cannot be certain that he is right, nor can he prove that he is. A posture of certainty on the analyst's part can only make it more difficult for the patient seriously to consider an alternative interpretation to his original one.[2]

THE NEW EXPERIENCE

It is important to recognize that the resolution of the transference in the here-and-now is accomplished not only by virtue of the examination of the relation between the patient's attitudes and the features of the actual analytic situation which serve as their point of departure, but also because in the very act of interpreting the transference the analyst behaves differently from what the patient has come to expect and even to provoke. Kanzer and Blum (1967), for example, write: "Although the analyst must retain an objective and dispassionate role, which insures against uncontrollable regression, his areas of sympathetic alliance with the patient in his sufferings and reliving activities inherently expand his functions beyond that of the object and interpreter of the transference neurosis and make him a participant in reliving experiences that revise the personality" (p. 125).

[2] I am indebted to Dr. Irwin Hoffman for this distinction between a plausible, though not unequivocally determined, hypothesis and a distortion.

Elsewhere Blum (1971) affirms Loewald's (1960) reference to the analyst as a "consistent and mature new object" and claims: "Even in adult analysis the role of the analyst as a real new object rather than the object of transference must be considered along with identification with the analyst and analytic attitudes" (p. 51).

This estimation of not only the inevitability but even the desirability of the new experience with the analyst seems counter to the analyst's reluctance to intervene in an effort to minimize the role of the analytic relationship as a factor in the result. Yet it is becoming increasingly recognized in our literature that the effects of an analysis are due not merely to insight but to the experience of a new relationship. Loewald's (1960) views on the important role the new relationship with the analyst plays in the analytic outcome have been accorded a generally favorable reception. Other analysts have also referred to the role of the new experience with the analyst as a mutative factor. Even Glover, the staunch advocate of "expectant" psychoanalysis and the analysis of the transference, asserts: *"The main function of the positive transference is indeed to permit a re-experience in non-ambivalent form of earlier ambivalent attitudes to the parents"* (1955, p. 128).

This new relationship is a very different matter from the deliberately engaged-in "corrective emotional experience" à la Alexander, for it is not a specific technical undertaking with the goal of influencing the patient. It is nevertheless inevitable that both the analyst's technical interventions and his personal, nontechnical relationship with the patient will be experienced by the patient as important interpersonal influences.

We can now clearly see the counterargument to the analyst's reluctance to make interventions lest the result be based on this interaction rather than on insight. Interaction is inevitable. If the analyst fails to analyze the interaction, he thereby increases the likelihood that whatever effects are achieved will be rooted in an unanalyzed interaction. The results of any analysis are a mixture in varying proportions of effects due to the analysis of the transference, to the accompanying new experience, and to the persisting transference. One must recognize that however expertly one analyzes the transference, the effect of an analysis will still, to a certain extent, be dependent on the gratification of the unanalyzed and persisting transference. One can only hope to make the outcome as dependent as possible on the analysis of the transference, with the inevitably accompanying new experience, and as independent as possible of persisting transference. It remains true, as Ferenczi (1909) quoted Freud as saying: *"we may treat a neurotic any way we like, he always treats himself psychotherapeutically, that is to say, with transferences"* (p. 55).

In summary, I advocate another shift in emphasis, in addition to giving priority to the analysis of resistance to the awareness of transference. Even after some aspect of the transference has been brought to awareness, instead of priority going to the resolution of such transference by relating it to contemporary or genetic extra-transference material, it should go to further work within the analytic situation. This includes both the elucidation of other aspects of the transference not yet in awareness, that is, further interpretation of resistance to the awareness of transference, and assessment of the transference attitudes in the light of the features of the actual analytic situation which serve as their point of departure, that is, interpretation promoting the resolution of transference. Both aspects of this work with the transference in the here-and-now require special attention to the features of the actual analytic situation. Robert Langs (1976, 1978) presents a point of view very similar to mine here. He refers to the features of the actual analytic situation as the "adaptive context."

8

TRANSFERENCE INTERPRETATION
IN THE HERE-AND-NOW VERSUS
GENETIC AND EXTRA-TRANSFERENCE
INTERPRETATIONS

It is historically interesting that in 1934 both Sterba's well-known article on "The Fate of the Ego in Analytic Therapy" and Strachey's article on "The Nature of Therapeutic Action" appeared in the same issue of the *International Journal of Psycho-Analysis*. Sterba essentially outlines the same two steps in transference interpretation that Freud (1912a) and Strachey do, though he shows the confusion between defense and resistance I described in arguing that the resistance is always expressed in the transference. Sterba writes:

> First of all, the analyst gives an interpretation of the defense, making allusion to the instinctual tendencies which he has already divined against which the defense has been set up. With the patient's recognition that his attitude in the transference is of the nature of a defense, there comes a weakening in that defense. The result is a more powerful onslaught of the instinctual strivings upon the ego. The analyst then has to interpret the infantile meaning and aim of these impulses. Ego dissociation and synthesis ensue, with the outcome that the impulses are corrected by reference to reality and subsequently find discharge by means of such modifications as are possible [p. 367].

The emphasis on the resolution of the transference by genetic interpretation, however, differs in the formulations of Freud, Sterba, and Strachey. Freud (1912a) refers to fitting the patient's emotional impulses into both "the nexus of the treatment and of his life-history" (p. 108). I take the first to mean transference interpretations in the here-and-now and the second to mean genetic transference interpretations. Sterba points clearly to interpreting the "infantile meaning" but refers to the "reality" of the analytic situation only ambiguously. Strachey speaks primarily of distinguishing the fantasy object and the real analyst, but he mentions, as a "corollary" to the two steps in a transference interpretation, the patient's obtaining "access to the infantile material which is being re-experienced by him in his relation to the analyst" (p. 34). Like Freud, he indicates that the genetic material will appear relatively easily and spontaneously after the resistance has been overcome.

Strachey's recognition of the importance of working through within the transference in the here-and-now may also be seen in his emphasis on the specificity necessary for a transference interpretation to be mutative. According to Strachey, a mutative interpretation must be both "detailed and concrete." Although the analyst may begin with less precise, more general interpretations, "it will be necessary eventually to work out and interpret all the details of the patient's phantasy system. In proportion as this is done the interpretations will be mutative" (p. 31). Strachey adds that to a great extent the need to repeat interpretations arises from the necessity of "filling in the details" rather than simply from the patient's id resistance. While Strachey's comments could be read as referring only to the progressive filling in of detail in the interpretations of the transference in the here-and-now, I believe he implies the filling in of details of the fantasy system by clarification, and perhaps interpretation, of extra-transference material too.

It should also be noted that in his emphasis on the filling in of details and working through Strachey offers an alternative to Freud's proposal of id resistance or what Freud calls the attraction of the infantile prototypes — a formulation I consider metaphorical and inferior to the formulation in terms of working through. I earlier criticized the concept of id resistance as confusing a source of resistance with its actual manifestation in the transference.

It is not that contemporary extra-transference and genetic transference interpretations have no value, but the danger is always that they will be employed as a flight from the immediacy of the transference within the analytic situation. They are the interpretations most likely to lend themselves to defensive intellectualization by both participants, and their repercussions on the transference may well be left unexamined. This is not to deny that contemporary and genetic material may have to be *clarified* and even interpreted to gain clues to understanding the transference. It is work with extra-transference material as such, without any reference to the transference, that I find questionable. In this sense, while Strachey may be correct that the majority of interpretations analysts actually make are outside the transference, I do not believe that this is true of the best analytic work.

Stone's views on the relative value of genetic and present transference interpretations are worth quoting. He indicates that too-quick genetic interpretations enhance resistance and that analysis of the transference in the here-and-now should take "precedence over genetic reduction." Yet, aside from those cases where the current conflict is avoided to such an extent that direct confrontation is the only approach, he believes that "ultimately, the genetic analysis of this conflict—in our immediate reference, the transference neurosis—will accomplish a type of understanding not otherwise available, which facilitates the stripping of transference illusion away from the person of the analyst" (1967, p. 46).

In another passage, however, Stone's emphasis comes much closer to mine. He, too, points out that what primarily convinces the patient that his transference is indeed transference is the detailed examination of the transference in the analytic situation rather than the recovery of memories of the past. He states: "Thus, to put it all too briefly, when hitherto structuralized impulses or general reaction tendencies can truly be accepted in terms of memory, i.e., as matters of the past, other than in a tentative explanatory sense, much of the analytic work with the dynamics of the transference neurosis has necessarily been accomplished. One does not readily give up a love or a hatred, personal or national, only because one learns that it is based on a crushing defeat of the remote past" (1973, p. 51).

It is generally recognized that any exclusive preoccupation on the analyst's part may skew the analytic process. A special interest in dreams, for example, may result in a change in the analysand's reporting of dreams or have other effects on the transference. So, too, will an exclusive interest in the transference provoke transference effects which themselves should become the subject of transference analysis. The possibility of an infinite regress presents itself. Indeed, an interpretation in the transference can have an effect on the transference that is the same as the content of the interpretation. The analyst may interpret, for example, that the patient takes the analyst's interpretations to be a seduction and the patient may take *that* interpretation to be a seduction. The analyst may be forced into a situation in which he seems reduced to silence, though he can of course also interpret that the patient seems motivated to reduce him to silence. This situation can arise with a patient who does not speak unless he feels urged to do so. He may interpret any intervention by the analyst as designed to thus urge him. Here, indeed, the analyst may have to be silent except to respond to what is clearly a spontaneous communication from the patient. While I have seen such a situation, I suspect it arises only if the analyst has for some time been engaged in an unrecognized and uninterpreted transference-countertransference interaction. When he then finally makes an interpretation, it still carries the interactive significance that the long-standing behavioral exchange has implicitly held. I also suggest that if such a situation arises, the analyst has not found the appropriate transference interpretation for the particular analytic situation. The analyst must find a transference which the patient cannot dismiss as totally explained by the present analytic situation.

Glover (1955) warns against the dangers of indiscriminate overemphasis on transference interpretation. He sees strict adherence to transference interpretation as an outright dismissal of "both theoretical and clinical considerations." While he does not deny the importance of transference interpretation to analytic work, he argues that "there is no need to stultify the practice of analysis by recommending its automatic application at all stages of all analyses" (p. 123). Here Glover underscores the variations in the impact of the patient's unconscious cathexes both within a single type of case and in different kinds of cases. *"The handling of the transference must therefore vary according to the man-*

ifestations existing in each case" (p. 123).

Glover goes on to insist: "we must be sure our transference-interpretations are reasonably correct" (p. 130). Incorrect transference interpretations may encourage the patient to develop a *"pseudo-transference-neurosis."* In such cases, the therapeutic effects are based on suggestion rather than on analytic work. And this, according to Glover, constitutes the danger of a "fetishistic" allegiance to transference interpretation. "It is true that from the time we commence transference-interpretation we can, if the occasion justifies it, interpret everything that happens in the analysis as a manifestation of transference. But we must not at any time convert our analytic technique into a rapport technique" (p. 130; see also p. 137).

I have already pointed out that whatever the analyst does is part of the actual situation and the patient's responses cannot be assumed to be uncontaminated transference. Glover ignores the principle I have stressed — that the effect on the transference of transference interpretations must also be analyzed. If an analysis in which the transference is being interpreted becomes a rapport therapy, it may mean the analyst has not been alert to the repercussions on the transference of his transference interpretations. As I pointed out earlier, this might be true of an analyst who aggressively interprets the transference without recognizing the repercussions of his interpretive activity on the transference. Nevertheless, I concede that the interpretation of these transference repercussions may itself fail because the very interpretation has the same repercussions. The truth of the assertion that the analyst cannot prevent the analytic situation from being an interpersonal one is once again demonstrated.

It is important that the analyst not be tied to some rigid rule that he should make only transference interpretations. Not only can extra-transference interpretations be useful, but the spontaneity of the analyst's behavior is essential for the conduct of an analysis. If an extra-transference interpretation occurs to the analyst as a plausible clarification, he should make it. At the same time, he should be alert to its possible repercussions on the transference — but then he should be alert to the repercussions on the transference of a transference interpretation too.

I conclude that while extra-transference interpretations play a role in analysis—and extra-transference clarification certainly must—priority, in both time and importance, should go to transference interpretations. This principle may be more readily accepted if I emphasize that attention to resistance to the awareness of transference should come first and that, even though priority in interpretation designed to resolve the transference should go to interpretation within the analytic situation, working through requires extra-transference, transference, *and* genetic transference interpretations. My criticism has been directed primarily against exclusively extra-transference interpretations, whether contemporary or genetic—that is, interpretations which are not made with an eye toward possible transference meanings.

A recent paper and book by Leites (1977, 1979) are worth reviewing because they make explicit the issues of the relative roles of transference and extra-transference interpretations, which, as Leites correctly states, have not been adequately discussed in our literature. I cannot agree with him, however, that there is a major trend toward emphasizing transference interpretations at the expense of extra-transference interpretations. Leites states that "transference has, to a substantial extent, reversed its direction. . . it travels no more only from parent to analyst, but also from the analyst to a person of the patient's past or present" (1977, p. 276). It is not that transference "travels" from the analyst to persons in the past or present but that associations about these persons may defensively include allusions to the transference which need to be made explicit. I believe that what Leites calls "disguised transference" (which I have referred to as resistance to the awareness of transference) is in fact often not adequately recognized and dealt with. Leites does not see that emphasis on the meaning for the transference of the patient's associations which are not manifestly about the transference is not intended to belittle their significance in the patient's life outside the treatment. It is not entirely clear what Leites's central message is. I think it may be to criticize what he believes is a tendency to make the analysis and the analyst too important in the patient's life. It is true that analysis may be perverted to an end rather than being a means. That can happen because of a countertransference or because of a failure to see that the patient is using the analysis as a defense against and substitute for life outside the analysis.

Freud wrote: "For, from the point of view of recovery, it is a matter of complete indifference whether the patient overcomes this or that anxiety or inhibition in the institution; what matters is that he shall be free of it in his real life as well" (1912a, p. 106).

The model I espouse is one in which the analysis of the transference *is* the analysis of the neurosis and in which the therapeutic effect is primarily the result of the combined cognitive and experiential accompaniments — both repetitive and new — of the examination of the transference. It is not one in which the analysis of the transference is ancillary to the analysis of the neurosis and in which the therapeutic effect is primarily the result of the cognitive recovery of the past.

Even some of those critics who are sympathetic to the emphasis I place on the analysis of the transference feel that I do not give enough weight to extra-transference and genetic transference interpretations. I am not convinced that this is so. In any case, I believe that analyses may differ widely in how they spontaneously gravitate to an emphasis on the present or on the past. Finally, I believe we need more experience and research with analyses conducted with the kind of emphasis on the transference for which I have argued.

9

KLEINIAN INTERPRETATION OF TRANSFERENCE

One of the reasons Kleinians have taken so much initiative in the interpretation of the transference is their conviction, similar to the one I have expressed and quoted from Freud, that the transference is often only implied in the patient's associations. Melanie Klein (1952) explains:

> For many years — and this up to a point is still true today — transference was understood in terms of direct references to the analyst in the patient's material. My conception of transference as rooted in the earliest stages of development and in deep layers of the unconscious is much wider and entails a technique by which from the whole material presented the *unconscious elements* of the transference are deduced. For instance, reports of patients about their everyday life, relations and activities not only give an insight into the functioning of the ego, but also reveal — if we explore their unconscious content — the defenses against the anxieties stirred up in the transference situation [p. 437].

When Hanna Segal (1967) writes that "the Kleinian analyst may be considered to follow the classical Freudian technique with the greatest exactitude, more so indeed than most other Freudian analysts who...alter their analytical technique... when dealing with pre-psychotic, psychotic, or psychopathic patients" (p. 169), it is essentially to the analysis of the transference that she is referring. She also notes that the analyst is the most important person in the patient's fantasies. In this light, she believes, one can see "that all communications contain something relevant to the transference situation" (p. 174). Segal thus agrees with my working assumption that all the patient's communications have an implication for the transference.

Zetzel (1956) offers a summary of the Kleinian point of view. She describes their approach as predicating therapeutic change on a shift in object relations as a result of transference interpretation. In her opinion, the Kleinians fail to distinguish clearly between "transference as therapeutic alliance and the transference neurosis as a manifestation of resistance. Therapeutic progress. . .depends almost exclusively on transference interpretation. Other interpretations, although indicated at times, are not, in general, considered an essential feature of the analytic process" (p. 171). Because of this, Zetzel indicates, the patient's initial ego strength plays less of a role in determining analyzability than it does in classical analysis.

Kleinians often say, as Segal (1967) does, that both the patient's fantasies and his current external life determine associations. Melanie Klein herself emphatically states that the analyst must pay just as much attention to the patient's current experience as to the early situations on which it is based. "In fact," she stresses, "it is not possible to find access to earliest emotions and object-relations except by examining their vicissitudes in the light of later developments. It is only by linking again and again (and that means hard and patient work) later experiences with earlier ones and vice versa, it is only by consistently exploring their interplay, that present and past can come together in the patient's mind" (1952, p. 437).

There is nevertheless a widespread belief that the patient's current external life as well as his current real relationship with the analyst do not figure much in Kleinian interpretations. Unfortunately, the fact that analytic reports so rarely give much of the raw data of the exchange makes it difficult to reach a firm conclusion on this point. In the Kleinian literature many of the reported transference interpretations are of primitive·fantasies, with little or no mention of the patient's real life either outside or within the analytic situation. Non-Kleinian analysts, on the other hand, see the transference attitudes as existing on a hierarchy from primitive to more reality-adapted, even if they are not of the opinion that an interpretation of the transference should take its point of departure from the reality of the analytic situation.

Here is an illustration of contradictory statements on the role of the reality of the analytic situation in the writings of Paula Heimann, a Kleinian analyst. In 1950, she pointed out that in considering the patient's repetition of past object experiences in the transference, the analyst must also evaluate his own role in, to some extent, provoking the patient's reactions. "He must be aware of himself, his personal peculiarities, etc., as prompting responses—both correct and distorted perceptions—in his patient which interact with the patient's spontaneous productions" (p. 307). But later, in 1962, she cites the assumption that innate envy and gratitude give rise to the defenses of splitting and projection, which lead to complex psychic processes. In recognizing the impact of these "instinctive" emotions, Heimann contends, the analyst must look to the importance of the early mother-child relationship for the analytic situation. And here she does suggest that "a crucial part of the analyst's task consists in following closely his patient's material as it refers to the analyst himself." Heimann then points to the Kleinian "shift in technique" evidenced in Segal's (1962) case presentation, where "the patient's actual fears and fantasies, based on his observations of the analyst, appear not to be very important for interpretation, whilst the analyst focuses on the patient's envy, splitting, and projection" (p. 231). This remark belittles the importance of the current real relationship with the analyst. Yet Heimann claims on the very same page that insight "will only be effective, if the experience includes the emotional change and *cathexis* that pertains to the immediate situation." And she reiterates: "All emotionally significant insight needs the stamp of present immediate reality, and this makes the analyst an important curative factor. He is in the dual roles of the patient's *transference-object* and *transference-self*" (p. 231).

I shall now discuss some illustrative Kleinian case vignettes to show how, although the reality of the analytic situation may be alluded to, it is used as the basis for a "deep" interpretation, without any indication of the bridging data which justify the conclusion reached.

Segal (1962) tells of a patient who dreamed that his flat was invaded by crowds of smokers. She states that in his associations to the dream there was a glaring omission: he made no reference to the fact that the analyst was a heavy smoker. She concludes from the dream that "the analyst is split into an external ideal object out of his reach, and the internal, greedy, dirty smokers" (p. 213). Heimann, in her discussion of the case, asks: "What does it mean that the patient has to use a *dream* to tell his analyst how much he feels he's persecuted by her smoking. . . ? I cannot believe that Segal did not pay attention to this exceedingly important transference content, yet in her interpretation she has not mentioned this part of the work at all" (1962, p. 230). Heimann goes on to disagree with Segal's interpretation that the dream reveals the splitting of the analyst into a persecutory figure and an idealized figure who is "out of reach." She notes that the only clear-cut reference to the analyst occurs in a detail of the dream, when the patient's wife tells him that she has gone to the analytic session in his place. According to Heimann, "The person who is split obviously. . . is the dreamer. . . . Thus to me the dream expresses in the transference the patient's fears of an oral, anal and phallic mother, from whom he must keep away his masculinity in order to protect his penis; it is only safe to present his feminine self to her. The glaring omission in his associations of any reference to the analyst's smoking suggests that in so presenting himself as feminine, he is to some extent pretending" (p. 230).

By pointing to the patient's failure to mention the analyst's heavy smoking, Segal seems to devote attention to the present reality. Yet her interpretation offers no bridge between the reality of her own smoking and the patient's alleged fantasy of a dirty, smoking, internal object. Heimann, in suggesting attention needs to be paid to the fact that the patient has to use a dream to tell his analyst how he feels about her smoking, also seems to emphasize current reality. But, while her interpretation differs from Segal's, no evidence is given for the complex speculation that the patient's lack of reference to the analyst's smoking indicates that the patient is spuriously presenting his feminine self to the analyst.

Another illustration from Segal is discussed by Greenson (1974) in his paper contrasting transference interpretation by Freudians and by Kleinians. Segal (1967) describes a candidate who started his first session with a declaration of his intention to qualify and, at the same time, "to get in all the analysis he could in the shortest possible time." After mentioning his digestive problems, this patient referred, in a different context, to cows. "He presented so clear a picture of his fantasy about the relation to the analyst," Segal asserts, "that I could, right then, make the interpretation that I was the cow, like the mother who breast-fed him, and that he was going to empty me greedily, as fast as possible, of all my analysis-milk. This interpretation immediately brought material about his guilt in relation to exhausting and exploiting his mother" (p. 175).

Greenson argues that the genetic material was not available for such an interpretation, and that the interpretation could have been only intellectually meaningful to the analysand, though it was correct to focus on the analysand's desire to get as much out of the analyst as quickly as possible. Again, while material relating to exploiting the mother does follow the interpretation, the cow is the slim clue that the analyst feels justifies her interpretation that the analytic situation is a repetition of the patient's breast-feeding. Furthermore, the analyst does not point to anything in the current analytic situation which would make it plausible to the patient that he feels he is greedily exploiting her and guilty for doing so.

In a reply to Greenson's paper, Rosenfeld (1974) contends that Greenson is not accurately stating the Kleinian position and offers an example of an interpretation in a first hour which is cogently and plausibly related to the immediate reality situation. Yet I believe that Greenson *is* correctly stating the essential Kleinian position, despite their statements and occasional illustrations which do seem to pay appropriate attention to current reality.

A variant of my criticism of transference interpretation that neglects the reality of the analytic situation is found in Glover's (1955) criticism of "transference interpretation isolated from the context of the patient's symptoms or character difficulties" (p. 75). He gives the example of how, based on previous anal-erotic reactions from an obsessional patient, the analyst may leap to the interpretation of an anal-erotic transference the first time the patient is late in paying his fee. What the analyst has done, Glover argues, is merely to "comment" on a characterological response without showing how this relates to the patient's early experience. As a result, the patient may miss the thrust of the interpretation and feel his integrity is being questioned. Moreover, he may see this remark as simply a reflection of the analyst's own worries about money. As Glover notes, "the unconscious symbolic equation of money and faeces is a well-established analytical fact. But the interpretation of symbolism in analysis is a means to an end: we should have that end clearly in view before we embark on the interpretation" (p. 75).

Nevertheless, I cannot agree that a transference interpretation should be made *only* in the context of the patient's symptoms or character. While I agree that a transference interpretation should not be made simply in terms of some theoretical premise the analyst has in mind, I would argue that the clarification of the immediate reality of the analytic situation is an adequate reason to make a transference interpretation.

Emphasis on the centrality of transference interpretation has become so closely linked with Kleinian technique and the Kleinian insistence on the crucial interpretation of preverbal phenomena that the former is sometimes considered as inevitably linked to the latter. Anna Freud (1969), for instance, underlines the controversy surrounding attempts "to carry analysis from the verbal to the preverbal period of development" (p. 146). Although she does not explicitly refer to Kleinianism, the implication seems clear.

Noting the differences in technique required to approach earlier as opposed to later phases of development, Anna Freud points to the emphasis on "the analyst's intuitive understanding of the patient's signs and signals." Because, as she indicates, neither memory nor verbal recall can reach back to the preverbal past, repetition and reenactment become important clues. "This," she believes, "explains the heightened significance of communication via the transference in many present-day analyses, where transference interpretations are considered the only therapeutic effective ones and where the transference phenomena are perforce given preference over memory, free association, and dreams, as the only real road to the unconscious" (p. 147).

And it is against "this central and unique role given to the transference in the psychoanalytic process, to the exclusion of all other avenues of communication," that Anna Freud argues. She criticizes the belief that the transference can in fact take the patient back to these earliest experiences. In her opinion, "it is one thing for preformed, object-related fantasies to return from repression and be redirected from the inner to the outer world (i.e., to the person of the analyst); but. . . it is an entirely different, almost magical expectation to have the patient in analysis change back into the prepsychological, undifferentiated, and unstructured state, in which no divisions exist between body and mind or self and object" (pp. 147–148).

I believe, on the contrary, that to give transference phenomena primary attention is not necessarily to give them "preference over memory, free association, and dreams," since these *all* provide clues to the transference, just as reenactment does. Nor does special attention to the transference necessarily mean special attention to inferences about preverbal development, as Anna Freud seems to imply.

From a different perspective, Strachey (1934), in propounding the mutative effectiveness of transference interpretations, focuses on superego transferences, that is to say, the patient's projections of superego attitudes onto the analyst. Again, I would not restrict transference interpretation to, or even single out, the analysis of superego aspects. Nevertheless, I do believe that Fenichel (1938–1939) has misread Strachey's paper in taking its central emphasis to be the introjection of the benign superego of the analyst. What Strachey is in fact highlighting is the interpretation of the transference.

It is interesting to see what Strachey, who was influenced by Melanie Klein, has to say about deep interpretations in this 1934 paper. He defines deep interpretations as "either genetically early and historically distant from the patient's actual experience or. . . under an especially heavy weight of repression — material, in any case, which is in the normal course of things exceedingly inaccessible to his ego and remote from it" (p. 29). In general, he believes such material is reached only late in an analysis and by degrees. I believe in effect this means the material is no longer distant from the patient's ego even if it is genetically early or was at one time heavily repressed — that is, it is no longer "deep" in the sense of being inaccessible to the patient's experience. In those occasional instances in which an impulse is urgent, although "deep" according to his definition, Strachey argues that whatever the danger of severe anxiety, a "deep" interpretation is safer than giving no interpretation; an interpretation of more superficial, nonurgent material; or reassurance. It seems very doubtful to me that the situation he describes ever actually arises — that is, that there can be an urgent impulse with no representation accessible to the patient's current experience.

My primary agreement with the Kleinian position is with its emphasis on the ubiquity of transference and the centrality and priority to be given to transference interpretation. My disagreement stems from the fact that, despite statements to the contrary, the Kleinians do seem to make inappropriately deep transference interpretations which fail to make adequate contact with the current reality of the actual analytic situation.

I believe the Kleinian emphasis on the transference may be one of the sources of its appeal to many analysts who implicitly or explicitly feel a lack of adequate attention to the transference in non-Kleinian analysis. Here, for example, is a case vignette from Pearl King (1962), a Kleinian, which not only illustrates careful attention to the transference but is also an example of an interpretation of identification in the transference. I referred earlier to the description of this phenomenon by Lipton (1977b) and how rarely it is made explicit in the writings on transference by Freudians.

> Let me give you an example from the analysis of a male patient whose main memory of his childhood is of wandering round his parent's house calling for his mother to play with him. He never remembered her doing so, and thought of her as being engrossed with housework, sewing, or reading. For months he treated me as this mother, complaining that I did nothing for him and asking me to put into him feelings and a zest for life. Interpretations were accepted as meaningful, and other material in the form of associations or dreams then followed to support the correctness of the interpretations. Nevertheless, the patient alternately complained and boasted that analysis had no effect on him, and said he completely shut it out at the end of the session. He said he could not 'think' about me or analysis — a shutter came down. After many

months I realized that I was feeling a bit exasperated, shut out, and useless, and started questioning my technique. It suddenly dawned on me, that while in terms of the verbal material the patient was giving me, I was clearly the mother who would not play with him (sexually), or feed him on demand; at the same time, in terms of his 'behavioural material' he had reversed the roles, so to speak, and I was being made to be and *feel* the child, and to experience what he had felt. I realized that it was my momentary feeling of exasperation that had given me the clue that had made it possible to re-orientate myself to the unconscious processes at work in this relationship within a transference relationship. . . . I could also show him that this was his unconscious way of trying to make me understand how he felt when his feelings were too muddled up to put into words, or were from a part of himself that he felt was cut off from words [King, 1962, p. 226].

This illustration very nicely portrays a number of features of good technique. The analyst comes to recognize how the current relationship with herself is an enactment not only of displacement in the transference (she is seen as the mother) but of identification as well (she is seen as the patient, while the patient becomes the mother). Her restricting herself to "proper" interpretation was probably equated by the patient with his mother's refusal to play, while his remaining unaffected by her analytic work was his refusal as the mother to play with the analyst (now himself). What King thus clearly shows us is the enactment of the transference by both parties in the current real relationship. In addition, she emphasizes how her feeling of exasperation (probably more than "momentary") was a clue she could use to recognize how the transference was being enacted. I doubt, however, that the patient resorted to behaving as he did because his feelings were "too muddled." Resistance to the awareness of transference is enough to explain his behavior.

I have wondered whether a reaction againt Kleinian analysis plays any significant role in the underemphasis on the transference in non-Kleinian analysis. That seems doubtful, however, if only because of the relative disregard of Kleinian writers by non-Kleinians (at least in most parts of the United States). Some of the most stimulating and instructive writing on the transference is by Heinrich Racker (1968), an Argentinian Kleinian, but it is not given much attention by non-Kleinians.

10

FREUD'S LEGACY

From a historical perspective, my claim is that the definitive technique of psychoanalysis was established by Freud soon after he abandoned directed association for free association, and catharsis for the analysis of resistance and transference — surely by 1900. Moreover, I would argue that although his application of these essential principles of technique may have improved, he did not change them in his lifetime, and that analytic technique has not improved since his death. Insofar as there has been a change, it has been in the progressive limitation of the analyst's responsiveness with the correlated overexpansion of what is encompassed in technique and the elevation of silence to a technique.

Ferenczi and Rank (1923) describe the major step made by Freud's technique over Breuer's cathartic method as Freud's recognition of "the fundamental importance of the transference." In their opinion, all subsequent advance in technique has merely elaborated on "this fundamental insight" (pp. 58–59).

Racker (1968) emphatically rejects the view that Freud's technique changed after the first decade of this century. He highlights Freud's active participation in his work with Dora (1905) and the Rat Man (1909b). What interests Racker "is that Freud interprets constantly, makes detailed and sometimes very extensive interpretations (speaking more or less as much as the patient), and the session is a straightforward *dialogue*. Those who link the concept of 'classical technique' with a predominance of a monologue on the part of the patient and with few and generally short interpretations on the part of the analyst, will have to

139

conclude, as I have said, that in this aspect Freud was not a 'classical' analyst" (p. 35).

Racker goes on to assert definitively that nowhere is there evidence that Freud later changed his technique or believed he should have acted differently. "While the contrary is not demonstrated to us, we have no ground whatever for thinking in a different way; while we do have grounds for maintaining that Freud did not depart in this respect from the technique he used in [his] early cases" (p. 35).

After reviewing all of Freud's writings after 1920 from the point of view of their implications for technique, Lipton (1967) concludes that Freud's "central preoccupation was not so much the development of psychoanalytic technique as its *preservation*" (p. 90). From this perspective, some alleged improvements are in fact departures from Freud's analytic technique, while others purport to be new but are in fact efforts to undo the departure. It is of interest that in his discussion of present-day technique, Lipton (1977a) comes to the same descriptive conclusion that Racker reaches, namely, that modern technique seems to have shifted from a dialogue, a conversation, to a monologue.

It is the personal relationship which Freud unabashedly engaged in with his patients that is the principal basis for the criticism of Freud's technique in our literature. Essentially this criticism takes the form of saying he should not have done the "nonanalytic" things he did with his patients. Such behaviors in the case of the Rat Man, for example, include feeding him, complimenting him, guessing at a thought the patient was having great difficulty in expressing, sending him a postcard, and asking to see a picture of his woman friend.

If this is indeed the primary basis for criticizing Freud's technique, there can hardly be any argument about whether his technique changed and improved. That Freud continued to engage in a personal relationship with his patients in addition to a technical one is evident from the accounts we have by Freud's analysands, which Lipton (1977a) points out show no difference from his behavior with the Rat Man (Wortis, 1954; Doolittle, 1956; Blanton, 1971; Riviere, 1939, 1956; Saussure, 1956; Alix Strachey [see Khan, 1973]; Kardiner, 1977).

Those who criticize Freud on this ground say that Freud failed to heed his own admonition of neutrality and was too interactive. They claim that the interactions in which he engaged resulted in his analyses being dependent to an unknown degree on effects of his personality (transference cure) — effects which he failed to analyze in the transference. In these critics' opinion, the contemporary, less interactive analyst is practicing a purer, more effective analysis. While I, too, shall argue that Freud did not analyze the transference as well as he might have, I do not ascribe this to his having a personal as well as a technical relationship with the patient. I have already expressed my view that a major trend in current practice is to expunge the personal relationship instead of recognizing it as part of the inevitably existing actuality of the analytic situation, which must be dealt with by analyzing its effects on the transference. The belief that something was amiss led to the concepts of the alliances and efforts to promote them, again as technical precepts. What has not been perceived is where the real problem lies, that is, the error of subsuming the entire relationship under technique and failing to analyze the effects of the actual situation on the transference.

TECHNIQUE SINCE FREUD

My perspective clashes with what I believe is a common belief among analysts that Freud continued to change and improve his technique during his lifetime, and that changes and improvements have continued since his death. There is a general air of steady progress, both in theory and technique, as though with time there must inevitably be improvements. The appearance of new terms like "therapeutic alliance" and "real relationship" is regarded as signaling new insights into and improvements of technique. Giving the lie to this general atmosphere are several explicit statements which affirm that the principles of technique have not undergone any essential change since Freud.

For example, Kanzer and Blum (1967) at first somewhat ambiguously claim that classical psychoanalysis has "continued [to evolve] consistently along structural lines since the death of Freud" and that Hartmann's contributions have influenced the clinical approach toward a greater emphasis on the ego's adaptive and self-regulatory functions (p. 138). Yet they point out that at its core classical analysis, both as theory and as therapy, "has undergone relatively little change." The change they see "is to be measured more in the analyst's outlook and use of his techniques than in their formal aspects" (pp. 138–139). Kanzer and Blum summarize the basic techniques as follows: "1. The induction and evolution of the transference neurosis in the analytic setting; 2. The organization of the patient-physician relationship by means of a verbal bridge, which makes interpretation the specific tool of the analyst and insight the effective force that initiates and guides therapeutic revisions in the personality" (p. 139).

Disagreement on whether technique has improved since Freud may to some extent hinge on questions of definition: (1) Should improvement in the application of a technique be considered a change in the technique itself? Though my contention is that the analysis of the transference was not carried out consistently by Freud, I do not define the difference as a change in technique. Some people might. I shall discuss this point in greater detail in connection with Kanzer's (1980) view that Freud's technique did not become definitive until after 1914 — after the cases of the Rat Man and the Wolf Man. (2) Should the explicit formulation of aspects of technique which had been taken for granted be considered an advance in technique? My position is not to regard this as such. I have indicated as much in discussing the actual relationship between the patient and the analyst and the therapeutic and working alliances. (3) Is it valid to make a distinction between increased knowledge of the human psyche and advances in technique? In "The Future Prospects of Psycho-Analytic Therapy" (1910b), Freud makes this distinction by dividing "internal progress" in the field into that in "analytic knowledge" and that in technique.

It is obvious that Freud continued to make contributions to our knowledge of the human psyche throughout his life. But "technique" refers not to the nature of the human psyche but to the basic principles of method for the conduct of an analysis. If the defense mechanisms are better understood now than they were in Freud's time, technique may be more effectively carried out, but that does not mean it has changed. Even such major shifts as the reappraisal of the relative importance of oedipal and preoedipal experience or of erotic and aggressive wishes occasion no change in technique as here defined. They only alert the analyst to kinds of contents he should see. Lipton (personal communication) has proposed the analogy of surgery. Asepsis is a standard part of surgical technique. The discovery of a new and better agent for asepsis is not a change in technique.

Changes in theory are to be distinguished from changes in technique. Even before 1900, Freud postulated that the defenses are unconscious. But what difference did it make for technique that, with the shift from the topographic to the structural theory, he ascribed them to the unconscious ego rather than to the *Ucs.*?

Hartmann (1951) writes of the technical implications of ego psychology. He, too, distinguishes between greater knowledge and advances in technique: "Genuinely technical discoveries — as was abreaction, and as was analysis of resistances — we do not find in the latest phase of analysis, but the body of systematic psychological and psychopathological knowledge has been considerably increased" (p. 32). According to Hartmann, new theory can facilitate the uncovering of facts, as well as the perception of the links between these facts. In other words, theory adds to knowledge and understanding. Hartmann, however, refers to the ramification for technique only as "a tendency toward more concrete, more specific interpretation" (p. 38).

In discussing ego psychology and interpretation in psychoanalytic therapy, Kris (1951) offers a similar observation. Pointing to structural theory and more recent conceptualizations of aggression and preoedipal conflicts, he notes: "A historical survey of the psychoanalytic literature would, I believe, confirm that these new insights were having reverberations in therapy, influencing, however, mainly the content of interpretation and not the technique of therapy in a narrower sense" (p. 18).

Glover (1931) makes much the same point. To counter the potential critic's argument that psychoanalysis is merely "another form of suggestion," Glover underlines the continuity in analytic technique. He stresses that the basic principles of therapy have remained the same, although knowledge — allowing for more complete interpretation—has expanded. According to Glover, "Analysis has always sought to resolve as completely as possible the affective analytic bond, both positive and negative. It has always pushed its interpretations to the existing maximum of objective understanding" (p. 361). Whatever the gaps in knowledge and thus the incompleteness in interpretation, analysis has always attempted "to loosen the bonds of repression" and "to head off all known protective displacements. In short, . . . it has never offered less than the known psychological truth" (p. 362). Glover concludes that the critics' attack on the adequacy of early analyses holds true only for "bad analysis" or "pseudo-analysis."

In the Preface to his book on technique (1955), Glover puts the same argument in a slightly different way. He points to the "natural limitations" to any expansion of technique. Although he acknowledges that increased knowledge of the factors involved in a particular disorder may lead to more specific and precise interpretation, Glover contends that "the analytic situation as such will continue to be governed by a few simple laws" (p. v). In his opinion, the patients, their disorders, and the analysts "do not change much." Nor is the course of the transference altered by advances in theory. The underlying principles of technique have not shifted. Thus Glover stresses: "No amount of interpretation nor any attempt to regulate the analytic situation according to the particular illness has any certain hope of success unless the fundamental movements in psycho-analysis are fully understood" (p. v).

A REVIEW OF FREUD'S DISCUSSIONS OF TRANSFERENCE

I have so far dealt with the establishment of Freud's definitive technique. My argument is that no significant changes took place in his technique after the basic principles of free association and analysis of the transference and resistance were articulated. I believe it can be shown, however, that although the centrality of transference analysis became progressively enunciated and hence presumably employed by Freud, his analysis of the transference never reached the primacy and centrality I hold it should have. To do so requires a review of his writings on transference.

I shall first examine his statements on the role of intellectual factors in the treatment because of my argument that the alternatives to transference analysis are to deal with the dynamics of the neurosis as displayed in the patient's contemporary life situation and/or to search for the memories of the past which explain the present. Insofar as these two approaches fail to deal with what is affectively immediate, I designate them as intellectualist.

In finding no relation between new theoretical views and a greater emphasis on reliving in the transference, Kris (1951) also seems to counterpose intellectualizing tendencies in analysis to transference analysis. Citing Freud's "conspicuous intellectual indoctrination of the Rat Man," Kris writes that this "was soon replaced by a greater emphasis on reliving in the transference, a shift which has no apparent direct relation to definite theoretical views" (p. 17). He sees the improved handling of the transference as arising not from "new theoretical insight," but rather from increased clinical experience. The comparison he draws is "to that process of a gradual acquisition of assurance in therapy which characterizes the formative decade in every analyst's development" (p. 18).

Although Lipton (1977a) disagrees with the view that the Rat Man case shows "conspicuous intellectual indoctrination," Freud himself admits that there were intellectualist aspects to his early technique—although how early is unclear (see 1913, p. 141). Indeed, Freud shows considerable ambivalence about working with the patient's intellect. He points out many times that the patient's intellectual knowledge of something is vastly different from his knowledge of it after the resistances to this knowledge have been resolved. Yet often in close juxtaposition to this devaluing of intellectual understanding as such, Freud indicates that suggesting a possibility to a patient can nevertheless serve as an "anticipatory idea," which will help him recover the repressed. In other words, Freud may criticize intellectualizing approaches and then propose that they serve a useful purpose— i.e., in setting the conflict in motion. A clear example of this ambivalence occurs in the case of Little Hans. Here Freud warns analysts against expecting to "cure the patient by informing him of this piece of knowledge." But in the same sentence, he mentions that the patient may "make use of [this information] to help himself in discovering the unconscious complex *where it is anchored* in his unconscious" (1909a, p. 121).

A similar example occurs in Freud's account of the treatment of the Rat Man (1909b). A passage appears in the text that might well be stamped as intellectualizing. Yet in a footnote Freud counters that the aim of such discussions is not to create conviction but "to bring the repressed complexes into consciousness, to set the conflict going in the field of conscious mental activity, and to facilitate the emergence of fresh material from the unconscious" (p. 181n). In another passage Freud explains that he told the patient "he ought logically to consider himself as in no way responsible for any of these traits in his character" (p. 185). Yet again, in a footnote, Freud criticizes such an intellectualizing approach: "I only produced these arguments so as once more to demonstrate to myself their inefficacy. I cannot understand how other psycho-therapists can assert that they successfully combat neuroses with such weapons as these" (p. 185n). Why did he have to demonstrate their inefficacy yet again? Was he not convinced?

In " 'Wild' Psycho-Analysis" (1910c), Freud points to the misconception "that the patient suffers from a sort of ignorance, and that if one removes this ignorance by giving him information. . . he is bound to recover. The pathological factor is not his ignorance in itself, but the root of this ignorance in his *inner resistances*" (p. 225). He then outlines two preconditions for giving this information: (1) that the patient himself be near the recovery of the repressed and (2) that the patient "have formed a sufficient attachment (transference) to the physician for his emotional relationship to him to make a fresh flight impossible" (p. 226).

In his "Recommendations" (1912b), Freud specifically tackles the question of seeking out the patient's intellectual comprehension. Although he sees the deliberate use of this cognitive understanding as varying according to the patient's personality, he advises "caution and self-restraint." To his mind, what the patient "has to learn above all — what never comes easily to anyone — [is] that mental activities such as thinking something over or concentrating the attention solve none of the riddles of a neurosis; that can only be done by patiently obeying the psycho-analytic rule" (p. 119). Here Freud points, in particular, to the need for strict adherence to the basic rule with patients who show a tendency to veer off into intellectual discussion. He also stresses his preference for his patients "to learn by personal experience" rather than resorting to analytic writings for assistance (pp. 119–120).

Yet, again in 1913, after describing how patients combine conscious knowing with not knowing, he adds that "the communication of repressed material to the patient's consciousness is nevertheless not without effect. It does not produce the hoped-for result of putting an end to the symptoms; but it has other consequences. At first it arouses resistances, but then, when these have been overcome, it sets up a process of thought in the course of which the expected influencing of the unconscious recollection eventually takes place" (p. 142). Later in the same paper, as I have already mentioned, he indicates the helpfulness of "the patient's intellectual interest and understanding." But he immediately goes on to clarify the restricted role of such intellectual understanding in the face of "the clouding of judgement that arises from the resistances" (p. 143).

A few years later, we find him saying: "How do we remove the resistance? . . . What are the motive forces that we work with? . . . First with the patient's desire for recovery . . . and secondly with the help of his intelligence, to which we give support by our interpretation" (1916–1917, p. 437).

Though this remark seems again to give some importance to intellectual factors, one of his last writings, "Analysis Terminable and Interminable," reads very differently: "we must not take the clarity of our own insight as a measure of the conviction we produce in the patient" (1937a, p. 229). In considering the stance that the patient's interest in inactive conflicts can be aroused "by talking to him about them and making him familiar with their possibility," Freud retorts: "The expected result does not come about. . . . We have increased his knowledge but altered nothing else in him" (p. 233). He compares this to what happens when one reads psychoanalytic writings: "The reader is 'stimulated' only by those passages which he feels apply to himself—that is, which concern conflicts that are active in him at the time. Everything else leaves him cold" (p. 233).

I suggest that the above remarks by Freud about the enlisting of the patient's intellect in the treatment show his vacillation between recognizing its relative inefficacy, on the one hand, and giving it a significant role, on the other. I believe that had he unequivocally embraced the centrality of transference interpretation, he would have resolved this vacillation in favor of a clear-cut relative deemphasis of the intellect per se in bringing about change.

I turn now to a chronological review of Freud's discussions of the analysis of the transference. Again, my argument is that although the centrality of transference analysis became progressively established, work on the transference remained ancillary to work outside the transference.

Transference is already described in *Studies on Hysteria* (Breuer and Freud, 1893–1895). Freud views the patient's transference onto the doctor as occurring through a "false connection," or "mésalliance." He believes that it is the patient's "compulsion to associate" that leads to the linking of the wish to the doctor. In other words, Freud does not yet see that the appearance of transference is connected to resistance. What he emphasizes is how this wish comes to be transferred because there are no conscious "memories of the surrounding circumstances which would [assign] it to a past time." Through the "false connection," then, "the same affect [is] provoked which had forced the patient long before to repudiate this forbidden wish" (p. 303).

Freud is, however, already on the way to recognizing the inevitability and universality of the transference. He remarks on its frequency (p. 302) and claims: "We can. . . reckon on meeting it in every comparatively serious analysis" (p. 301). He even begins to recognize that the transference is not as great an obstacle as he at first thought: "To begin with I was greatly annoyed at this increase in my psychological work [because of the transference], till I came to see that the whole process followed a law; and I then noticed, too, that transference of this kind brought about no great addition to what I had to do" (p. 304).

Freud's next discussion of transference, in the Dora case (1905), reveals that though he now has what is doubtless close to his definitive understanding of it in technique, his understanding is not yet secure, for the patient's flight from the treatment may have been due to his failure to analyze the transference in time. He writes that "the transference took me unawares and, because of the unknown quantity in me which reminded Dora of Herr K., she took a revenge on me as she wanted to take her revenge on him, and deserted me as she believed herself to have been deceived and deserted by him" (p. 119).

As Muslin and I (1978) have pointed out, the Dora case contains, side by side, indications that Freud still regards the transference as an obstacle and indications that he now sees the full importance of transference analysis. Evidence of the former view can be found in Freud's statement: "I was deaf to this first note of warning, thinking I had ample time before me, since no further stages of transference developed and the material for the analysis had not yet run dry" (p. 119). There had actually been many more manifestations of the transference than this "first note," and to say that "the material for the analysis had not yet run dry" is to believe that analytic work can proceed, even if only for a time, without attention to the transference.

Yet another indication that Freud still pictures the transference as an obstacle is his contention: "When it is possible to work transference into the analysis at an early stage, the course of the analysis is retarded and obscured, but its existence is better guaranteed against sudden and overwhelming resistances" (p. 119). To say that the analysis is "retarded and obscured" clearly shows the peripheral role ascribed to work with the transference.

Another indication that the transference has not yet been accorded a central role is Freud's description (in the Dora case) of dreams as standing "upon two legs, one of which is in contact with the main and current exciting cause, and the other with some momentous event in the years of childhood" (p. 71). The context makes clear that by "current exciting cause" he means something extraneous to the analytic situation. But we might conjecture that, with his later understanding of transference, he would have written that the dream of an analysand has a third leg in the transference.

With regard to the second view, we find evidence in the "Postscript" to the Dora case that Freud has begun to move from considering the transference an obstacle to regarding it as an unavoidable and necessary feature of analytic work. Clearly reversing his earlier view, Freud asserts: "Transference, which seems ordained to be the greatest obstacle to psycho-analysis, becomes its most powerful ally, if its presence can be detected each time and explained to the patient" (p. 117). He also notes that "it is only after the transference has been resolved that a patient arrives at a sense of conviction of the validity of the connections which have been constructed during the analysis" (pp. 116–117).

In summary, we can say that in the Dora case the transference indeed took Freud "unawares" and led to a "sudden and overwhelming resistance," for Freud was so intent on studying the patient's intrapsychic dynamics and her developmental history that he was blind to the many manifestations of transference in his ongoing interaction with Dora. Had he given these their proper place, the analysis would have been hastened and clarified, not "retarded and obscured."

The next writing from which we can learn Freud's views on the analysis of the transference is his report of his analysis of the Rat Man (1909b). Opinions about his work in this case differ widely. The reason is not far to seek. Because the case report is not intended as a study of technique, one can only glean ideas about Freud's technique from bits here and there, bits sufficiently ambiguous that the text is practically a projective test instrument for writers on technique. One might have thought that one would learn much more about Freud's technique through the discovery of a batch of his notes on the case (1909b, pp. 259–318), but the notes are as subject to varying interpretation as the official case report.

My own view is essentially in agreement with Lipton's (1977a) contention that Freud's technique in this case represents his definitive technique and that it has advantages over much of present-day technique. I have already indicated my support of Lipton's view that Freud's willingness to have a personal relationship with his patient, apart from his technical activity, is preferable to the current effort to subsume the entire relationship under technique. I believe, however, that the Rat Man case shows that Freud did not interpret the transference as fully and consistently as I argue it should be.

Muslin (1979a) takes a view intermediate between those who, like Lipton, admire Freud's technique with the Rat Man and those who are critical of it. Muslin, like myself, sees much to question in Freud's handling of the transference in this case, but he describes Freud's technique here as transitional, moving toward a presumed later improvement (although he admits that there is no clear evidence that Freud did in fact ever analyze the transference any differently from his work with the Rat Man).

A major difficulty in assessing Freud's technique in the Rat Man case is that one does not know how much importance to attach to what he seems not to have done. The fact that Freud did not write this report to demonstrate technique means that a failure to mention something does not necessarily mean that he didn't do it. Nevertheless, I would argue that my criticism that Freud failed to analyze the transference adequately is valid because there are striking instances in which it is hard to believe that he would not have noted the results of examining the transference had he indeed done so.

The primary criticisms of Freud's technique, however, rest on things he admits doing which are allegedly violations of technique, including his "infamous" report that he once gave the Rat Man something to eat. It is this sort of thing that has led critics like Kanzer (1980) and Beigler (1975) to argue that, as Kanzer puts it, Freud used the transference as "human influence" to get the patient to give up his resistances. My objection is not that Freud did these things but that, in my opinion, he did not always analyze their repercussions on the transference.

On the other hand, there *is* a very neat example in the case in which Freud does interpret the repercussions on the transference of the most commonly cited "violation" of correct technique, namely, the feeding. The patient subsequently reported a fantasy about two women and a herring, which Freud traces to the meal. Even more strikingly, Freud interprets a detail in the fantasy as referring to a remark Freud had made some time before — a remark, incidentally, which is likely to make adherents of "proper" technique blanch. Freud attributes the fact that the women in the fantasy have no genital hair to his response to the patient's description of how his girlfriend had lain on her stomach so that her genital hairs could be seen from behind. He had replied that "it was a pity that women nowadays gave no care to them and spoke of them as unlovely" (p. 311).

Kanzer (1980) regards the Rat Man case as revealing a very early stage of Freud's understanding of transference. He bases his view that Freud's technique must have changed drastically after the Rat Man on various formulations in the technical papers of 1911–1915, in particular, on those which bring current reality into the picture. Here Kanzer cites Freud's statement that "we must treat his illness, not as an event of the past, but as a present-day force" (1914, p. 151). Yet in his next sentence Freud remarks that "while the patient experiences it as something real and contemporary, we have to do our therapeutic work on it, which consists in a large measure in tracing it back to the past" (p. 152) — a comment that, in my view, is still in the vein of the primary analysis of the transference in terms of the past.

In his paper on "The Future Prospects of Psycho-Analytic Therapy" (1910b), written after the Rat Man case and before the papers on technique, Freud says two things which at first seem to confirm Kanzer's view. He speaks of "the intellectual help which makes it easier for [the patient] to overcome the resistances between conscious and unconscious" and continues: "Incidentally, I may remark that it is not the only mechanism made use of in analytic treatment; you all know the far more powerful one which lies in the use of the 'transference' " (p. 142). But this is the same use of transference which Freud has described earlier and will again later. It refers to the use of the (unobjectionable positive) transference to overcome resistance. In Freud's view, this is in no way inconsistent with the simultaneous analysis of transference resistance.

One of the reasons that some analysts reach the mistaken conclusion that Freud's technique underwent continuing development after the first decade of this century is that those papers which come closest to being a textbook on technique were not written until between 1911 and 1915. The assumption is that technique must have been developing during this time just as theory was.

Yet in these papers we still find evidence of the conceptualization of transference as an obstacle in the frequent references to hypnosis as a model. Freud describes, for example, the "ideal remembering of what has been forgotten which occurs in hypnosis [and] corresponds to a state in which resistance has been put completely on one side" (1914, p. 151). Here Freud compares the easy retrieval of memories in the early stages of the positive transference to that under hypnosis. This "ideal remembering" shifts to acting out and the patient's defending himself "against the progress of treatment" once "the transference becomes hostile or unduly intense" (p. 151).

The above remarks occur in Freud's essay on "Remembering, Repeating and Working-Through" (1914). The paper begins with a historical review of the development of Freud's technique. Freud identifies the first step as Breuer's cathartic method, in which directed association was used in the hypnotic state to bring about remembering and abreaction. The next stage entailed giving up hypnosis and discovering from the patient's free associations what he failed to remember. During this stage, according to Freud, the resistance was to be circumvented by the work of interpretation and making its results known to the patient, although the symptom and related situations remained the focus of interest. (I would point out that in this case the associations were hardly permitted to be free.) In the third, the current stage that Freud depicts here, the analyst no longer attempts "to bring a particular moment or problem into focus. He contents himself with studying whatever is present for the time being on the surface of the patient's mind, and he employs the art of interpretation mainly for the purpose of recognizing the resistances which appear there, and making them conscious to the patient" (p. 147).

This sketch of the development of technique is confined to how the search for memories first started from a fixed point but then had to take the circuitous route through the patient's free associations and the interpretation of resistance. No explicit mention of transference is made here. But Freud goes through this delineation of stages to prepare for the central point of his paper — that the search for memories alone will not suffice because much of the past is enacted, that is, repeated in action, rather than remembered in ideas, and this acting out (repetition) constitutes the transference.

While analysts generally consider that Freud's views on transference are the same throughout the technical papers of 1911–1915, Kanzer (1966) advances the interesting suggestion that these six papers should be divided into two sets: (1) the paper on dream interpretation (1911a), the one on "The Dynamics of Transference" (1912a), and the first two papers of recommendations on technique (1912b, 1913); (2) the paper on "Remembering, Repeating and Working-Through" (1914) and the "Observations on Transference-Love" (1915). He believes that only in the second set does Freud take adequate account of action and reality. In line with this, Kanzer notes that the shift between the two sets coincides with the break with Jung and with the first draft of the paper on narcissism, which to Kanzer signals the "reorientation of psychoanalysis from a depth psychology to an ego psychology, correlating inwardly and outwardly directed interests" (p. 528).

I do not agree with Kanzer that this major shift takes place in the paper on "Repeating, Remembering and Working-Through." Instead, I agree with James Strachey, who indicates in a footnote to "The Dynamics of Transference" that Freud is already stating here an idea which becomes elaborated in "Remembering, Repeating and Working-Through." The relevant passage in the earlier paper is: "The unconscious impulses do not want to be remembered in the way the treatment desires them to be, but endeavour to reproduce themselves in accordance with the timelessness of the unconscious and its capacity for hallucination," that is, "as contemporaneous and real" (1912a, p. 108). In fact, as Strachey points out in another footnote (1914, p. 150n), Freud already stated the concept of "acting out" in this same sense in the case of Dora. He wrote about Dora's leaving treatment: "Thus she *acted out* an essential part of her recollections and phantasies instead of reproducing it in the treatment" (1905, p. 119).

Kanzer believes his argument is borne out by his interpretation of Freud's sketch of three stages of the development of technique in *Beyond the Pleasure Principle* (1920a). According to Freud, at first the analyst "could do no more than discover the unconscious material that was concealed from the patient, put it together, and, at the right moment, communicate it to him. Psycho-analysis was then first and foremost an art of interpreting" (1920a, p. 18). In the second stage, it became necessary for "the patient to confirm the analyst's construction from his own memory." The analyst then concentrated on uncovering the patient's resistances and "inducing him by human influence—this was where suggestion operating as 'transference' played its part—to abandon his resistances" (p. 18). Because the patient has to repeat much of what is repressed rather than simply remember it, the analysis of the transference neurosis became a central feature of technique in the third phase. Here, in contrasting repetition to remembering, Freud refers to his 1914 paper. He does not, however, give any dates for these three stages.

Kanzer concludes that Freud's reference in 1920 to the paper of 1914, plus the fact that the term "transference neurosis" rather than simply "transference" appears for the first time in the paper of 1914, means that Freud did not definitively understand and utilize the analysis of the transference neurosis until 1914. He suggests that until then the transference was used suggestively to persuade the patient to overcome his resistances, and, as I have already pointed out, he believes Freud's technique with the Rat Man justifies this view.

I believe Kanzer is mistaken. The use of transference as suggestion to induce the patient to abandon his resistance, as I pointed out in connection with the Rat Man case (1910b), refers to a very early and *continuing* use of transference. It was not given up when Freud began to analyze the transference.

Freud cites the 1914 paper in the 1920 monograph because he is developing the theme of the repetition compulsion and the 1914 paper is the one in which he spells out in detail the connection between repeating and remembering. Furthermore, Freud never makes much of the distinction between "transference" and "transference neurosis" which I discussed earlier—the term "transference neurosis" hardly appears again after its introduction. The reason may well be that for Freud the term is preempted for its other use—a neurosis in which the patient is capable of forming a workable transference—a use that occurs at least half a dozen times in *The Introductory Lectures* (1916-1917).

I reaffirm my view then that Freud's definitive technique was established very early, surely by 1900, and that the third stage described in this review of 1920 was reached very early in the history of psychoanalysis. I believe that Kanzer is reading into the papers on technique an understanding and use of transference equal to the best technique employed today, which Freud never attained. This is not to say, however, that Freud's understanding and practice of the analysis of transference did not advance as his experience grew.

The case of the Wolf Man was completed in 1914 (although published only in 1918), and it is reasonable to suppose that Freud's practice with the Wolf Man and his views on the technical papers of 1911–1915 should be the same. Kanzer (1980), however, believes that "Remembering, Repeating and Working-Through" (1914) offers an advance beyond the technique used with the Wolf Man because of what Freud had learned after beginning that case. The primary obstacle to knowing how Freud dealt with the transference in the case of the Wolf Man is that he tells us almost nothing directly about it. Freud's write-up is avowedly not intended as a study of the process. It is a report of the yield of the process, and even then it is primarily restricted to a particular aspect of that yield, namely, the infantile neurosis.

Any study of the process in the case thus seems to come up against insuperable barriers. Surely it is inappropriate to tax Freud with the omission of this or that when he explicitly disavows that he is telling us what went on in the process. Mindful of this objection, I am nevertheless of the opinion that, as with the Rat Man case, there is significant indirect evidence of how the analysis was conducted. I believe it is important to focus on this evidence because, in my opinion, Freud conducted the case in a way which is not in accord with what I consider the best practice to be.

I believe there is good evidence that the primary focus of the work was not on the transference but on the dynamics of the neurosis. The transference was apparently still, to a significant extent, considered an impediment to analytic work, whatever recognition there was of its inevitability and indispensability. Freud notes: "Whenever he shrank back onto the transference from the difficulties of the treatment, he used to threaten me with eating me up" (1918, pp. 106–107). While this remark is decidedly a recognition of transference as resistance, it clearly implies that the real work lies outside the transference. I agree with Muslin (1979b) that the mutative factors are explicitly stated to be the material recovered, without any reference to the development and resolution of a transference neurosis. Freud explains that "the analysis produced all the material which made it possible to clear up his inhibitions and remove his symptoms" (1918, p. 11).

Of course I am not suggesting that Freud did not work with the transference. But the question is one of emphasis and precedence. Against the possible argument that when Freud speaks of the material which enabled him to "clear up his inhibitions and remove his symptoms" he means the material in the transference, I offer this additional statement about the significant factors in the cure: "All the information, too, which enabled me to understand his infantile neurosis is derived from this last period of work, during which resistance temporarily disappeared and the patient gave an impression of lucidity which is usually obtainable only in hypnosis" (p. 11). This is indeed a remarkable statement by the discoverer of the unavoidability of resistance if significant work is to be accomplished. And it is even more remarkable in the light of this assertion: "Hypnosis conceals the resistance and renders a certain area of the mind accessible; but as against this, it builds up the resistance at the frontiers of this area into a wall that makes everything beyond it inaccessible" (1910a, p. 26).

But perhaps the most persuasive evidence that the transference was not given its due is Freud's resort to the device of setting a time limit, which he himself labels "blackmailing." He tells us that what led him to this extremity was the patient's continuing to hide "behind an attitude of obliging apathy" (1918, p. 11). This is the kind of attitude which presumably all analysts would now agree should become the focus of intensive work in the transference, but Freud does not say that it did. Whether or not it did or to what extent it did, the fact remains that Freud does tell us he dealt with it by a manipulation. Again, recognizing that the ice becomes thin when I say he didn't do something on the grounds that he doesn't say he did, it seems to me highly improbable that he could have remained totally silent about an analysis of the meaning in the transference of this blackmailing device had he indeed analyzed it.

Furthermore, he explicitly tells us that he did manipulate the transference. He states: "I was obliged to wait until his attachment to myself had become strong enough to counterbalance this shrinking and then played off this one factor against the other" (p. 11). This is the same proposal he makes in his paper on "Lines of Advance in Psycho-Analytic Therapy" (1919), in which he writes about "severe cases of obsessive acts": "I think there is little doubt that here the correct technique can only be to wait until the treatment itself has become a compulsion, and then with this counter-compulsion forcibly to suppress the compulsion of the disease" (p. 166). This is a recommendation for transference manipulation, not analysis. The suggestion has faded away; it has not come to occupy any acceptable place in analytic technique.

Another avenue to understanding the role of transference in Freud's work with the Wolf Man, again admittedly indirect, is the subsequent work which Ruth Mack Brunswick (1928) did with him. That her primary work with the Wolf Man concerned his transference to Freud is an indication of what was omitted in Freud's work with him. But even she writes that "one fact supports our assumption that the patient did not finish his reactions to the father" (p. 304). The focus is on the father, not the transference. Also striking is the fact that her focus was on the transference to Freud; we learn little about the Wolf Man's transference to *her*. Even *her* emphasis on the transference, then, is one step removed.

I am deliberately refraining from speculating on just what the transference was, though there is plenty of material for speculation. If one were to speculate about the transference, one should look for a transference which was expressed to both Freud and Brunswick. I believe such speculation would detract here from the central point I wish to make. It is in some ways unfortunate that the case of the Wolf Man plays such a prominent role in the training of analysts because it encourages an underemphasis on the process, specifically on the transference in the process, and an overemphasis on the yield. Despite Freud's explicit statement that his report is designed only to describe the infantile neurosis, the student may well be influenced to underemphasize the process.

I do wish to say a word about the countertransference, however, as I believe Freud's work with the Wolf Man may not have been typical of his practice at the time because of important countertransference issues. Freud tells us at the outset that he had an important aim in mind, quite apart from the analysis of the Wolf Man. He points out that the case history was written down shortly after the termination of the treatment, when he was "still freshly under the impression of the twisted re-interpretations which C. G. Jung and Alfred Adler were endeavouring to give to the findings of psycho-analysis" (1918, p. 7n). It is a reasonable assumption that in the conduct of the case itself he was seeking conclusive data to refute these "twisted re-interpretations" and that this deflected him from the transference.

A countertransference is also suggested by how Freud behaved later toward the Wolf Man. I refer to the annual collections and the continuing free treatment by others. Indeed, one might even suggest that the entire analytic community has a countertransference toward the Wolf Man.

The Wolf Man is generally considered to have suffered from a severe disorder with important narcissistic features. His ideas about his nose are close to delusional, if not definitely so. I am not impugning the therapeutic results achieved with him. I am not even implying that the results would necessarily have been better had the transference been better analyzed. But I am saying that there are clear indications that the transference did not occupy the role in the process which I maintain it should in a well-conducted analysis.

The difficulty one encounters in assessing how the transference has been dealt with unless one has detailed knowledge of what went on is exemplified in one of Freud's lesser-known cases. The report is on "The Psychogenesis of a Case of Homosexuality in a Woman" (1920b). In it Freud describes how the patient's vengeful feelings toward her father "made her cool reserve possible." He then goes on to comment on the seeming lack of transference to the analyst. Yet he immediately corrects this observation by pointing out that there must always be "some kind of relation to the analyst. . . and this relation is almost always transferred from an infantile one." In this case the transference lies in the patient's rejection of all men ever since an early disappointment by her father. Yet, instead of calling attention to the need to analyze such a negative transference, Freud seems to sidestep the issue:

> Bitterness against men is as a rule easy to gratify upon the physician; it need not evoke any violent emotional manifestations, it simply expresses itself by rendering futile all his endeavours and by clinging to the illness. I know from experience how difficult it is to make a patient understand just precisely this mute kind of symptomatic behaviour and to make him aware of this latent, and often exceedingly strong, hostility without endangering treatment. As soon, therefore, as I recognized the girl's attitude to her father, I broke off the treatment and advised her parents that if they set store by the therapeutic procedure it should be continued by a woman doctor [p. 164].

To question Freud's experience would seem to be presumptuous, but to fail to do so is to rely solely on his authority. In fact there is some evidence that he did make some attempt to analyze the negative transference, even in this patient. He describes, for example, his disbelief in a series of dreams the patient had which were contrary to her waking utterances. After pointing out to the patient the "falseness" of her dreams and her attempt "to deceive [the analyst] just as she habitually deceived her father," these particular dreams stopped. But, while proclaiming the correctness of his interpretation, Freud goes on to state: "I still believe that, beside the intention to mislead me, the dreams partly expressed the wish to win my favour; they were also an attempt to gain my interest and my good opinion — perhaps in order to disappoint me all the more thoroughly later on" (p. 165).

Is it only coincidence that these words are so similar to those he used to explain what he felt might have happened had he tried to persuade Dora to remain in treatment? Is it possible that a particular countertransference was at work? Or that Freud would have experienced more success in analyzing such a transference had he done it differently? What he says he told this patient about her dreams, for example, seems abrupt, without any bridge to evidence for the interpretation drawn from the actual analytic situation. And did he examine the meaning in the transference of the cessation of these dreams after his interpretation?

Freud's discussion of transference in the *Introductory Lectures* (1916–1917) is much the same as in the papers on technique. But he does use the term "transference neurosis" in a way which comes closer than any previous formulation to giving the transference neurosis the central role in technique. As we have already noted, he asserts: "When the transference has risen to this significance ["the whole of his illness's new production is concentrated upon a single point—his relation to the doctor"], work upon the patient's memories retreats far into the background" (p. 444).

There are no indications in Freud's writings after the *Introductory Lectures* that his view on the analysis of transference changed. Chapter 5 of *The Question of Lay Analysis* (1926b), for instance, includes a footnote by Strachey stating: "Much of the material in this chapter is derived, in some passages almost word for word, from Freud's earlier papers on technique" (p. 228n). While this probably means that Freud's views were unchanged, Lipton (1967) cautions that one must remember that this book was written for lay consumption. The monograph contains this remarkably terse summary of analytic technique: "The analyst agrees upon a fixed regular hour with the patient, gets him to talk, listens to him, talks to him in his turn and gets him to listen" (p. 187).

That Freud had lost the optimism about improving analytic technique that he had hinted at in "Lines of Advance in Psycho-Analytic Therapy" (1919) may be seen in this passage from *The Question of Lay Analysis*: "I am unfortunately obliged to tell you that every effort to hasten analytic treatment appreciably has hitherto failed. The best way of shortening it seems to be to carry it out according to the rules" (1926b, p. 224).

Several years later, in 1933, near the end of his life, he states the limitations of psychoanalysis even more emphatically:

> The therapeutic ambition of some of my adherents has made the greatest efforts to overcome these obstacles so that every sort of neurotic disorder might be curable by psycho-analysis. They have endeavoured to compress the work of analysis into a shorter dura-

tion, to intensify transference so that it may be able to overcome any resistance, to unite other forms of influence with it so as to compel a cure. These efforts are certainly praiseworthy, but, in my opinion, they are vain. They bring with them, too, a danger of being oneself forced away from analysis and drawn into a boundless course of experimentation [p. 153].

Since the reader may well class me among those with overweening therapeutic ambition, I note that I do not suggest that all psychopathology is curable. Nor am I advocating compressing the work of analysis, intensifying the transference, or uniting other forms of influence with it. What I do support is greater attention to allusions to the transference and to the role of the actual analytic situation in analyzing the transference.

In his *New Introductory Lectures* (1931, p. 151), Freud also indicates that his theoretical formulations on psychoanalytic technique have already been presented in his *Introductory Lectures* (1916–1917) and that they have not changed since then. And, in fact, we find relatively little and nothing new about the analysis of the transference in Freud's late, summarizing work "An Outline of Psycho-Analysis" (1940).

It is usually said that the paucity of Freud's writings on technique is due to his unwillingness to lay down rules in a situation so variable that it cannot be dealt with mechanically—that he believed the analyst's personality must inevitably play an important role in this situation and hence his behavior should not be prescribed. In contrast to the emphatic statements cited above, for example, he writes of his decision "to call [his] rules 'recommendations' and not to claim any unconditional acceptance for them" (1913, p. 123). Noting the diversity of psychic characteristics and the multiplicity of factors involved in any illness, Freud points out that no single rule can be effective in every case. The guidelines he proposes are ones that are "effective on the average" (p. 123). Elsewhere, he points out: "what I am asserting is that this technique is the only one suited to my individuality; I do not venture to deny that a physician quite differently constituted might find himself driven to adopt a different attitude to his patients and to the task before him" (1912b, p. 111).

It is difficult to know how thoroughly and systematically, as well as exactly how, Freud did analyze the transference in his work. One reason, as I have already indicated, is that Freud's case reports are not such as to enable one to see the details of his technique and, in particular, his analysis of the transference. He was more interested in presenting the dynamics of the neurosis and felt that it would be impossible to give the mass of detail necessary to show the analytic work. He never wrote a comprehensive or extensive study of technique, and his technical writings are a small fraction of his output. Especially striking in this regard is the fact that the Fliess letters (1887–1902), which cover the period of the change from catharsis to psychoanalysis, are almost devoid of any mention of technique, though they include detailed discussions of even the transitory and soon-to-be-discarded ideas in Freud's development of theory.

That a description of technique is not a major concern in any of Freud's case reports is stated explicitly by Freud himself. Obviously in the cases of Little Hans (1909a), who was not treated directly by Freud, and Schreber (1911b), who was analyzed only from his autobiography, we cannot even expect to learn about his handling of the transference. I shall not, therefore, consider those cases here.

In the case of Dora (1905), Freud explains that aside from his discussion of dreams, little is revealed about his analytic technique.

> My object in this case history was to demonstrate the intimate structure of a neurotic disorder and the determination of its symptoms; and it would have led to nothing but hopeless confusion if I had tried to complete the other task at the same time. Before the technical rules, most of which have been arrived at empirically, could be properly laid down, it would be necessary to collect material from the histories of a large number of treatments. Nevertheless, the degree of shortening produced by the omission of technique is not to be exaggerated in this particular case. Precisely that portion of the technical work which is the most difficult never came into question with the patient; for the factor of 'transference', which is considered at the end of the case history, did not come up for discussion during the short treatment [p. 13].

That it is in connection with the discussion of this case, in which the transference was hardly dealt with at all, that Freud makes his first major statement about transference lends some credence to Kanzer's (1980) idea, expressed in connection with the Rat Man, that Freud's increased understanding of technique derives more from his experience in the case, rather than from its having been actually employed in the case.

In the case of the Rat Man (1909b), Freud comments that if he were to detail the analytic work per se, it would become impossible for the reader to see the neurotic structure "through the mass of therapeutic work superimposed upon it" (p. 156). A year later Freud makes a similar remark: "I need not rebut the objection that the evidential value in support of the correctness of our hypothesis is obscured in our treatment as we practise it to-day; you will not forget that this evidence is to be found elsewhere, and that a therapeutic procedure cannot be carried out in the same way as a theoretical investigation" (1910b, p. 142).[1] Indeed, these words echo the statements from the Dora case: "When it is possible to work transference into the analysis at an early stage, the course of the analysis is retarded and obscured" (1905, p. 119).

In the case of the Wolf Man (1918), Freud stresses: "Only this infantile neurosis will be the subject of my communication" (p. 8). He goes on to offer a disclaimer for his omission of a detailed report of the treatment method: "It is well known that no means has been found of in any way introducing into the reproduction of an analysis the sense of conviction which results from the analysis itself. Exhaustive verbatim reports of the proceedings during the hours of analysis would certainly be of no help at all; and in any case the technique of the treatment makes it impossible to draw them up" (p. 13). As should be clear from my remarks in the Introduction, I disagree with these last two assertions.

One of the few instances in which one can see details of Freud's technique occurs in the *New Introductory Lectures* (1933) — in the case material relating to thought transference in connection with the name "Forsyth" (pp. 47–54). The discussion illustrates resistance to the awareness of transference. This resistance is displayed in three associations given by the patient during the

[1] Earlier (p. 90), I discussed this statement in relation to Freud's distinction between therapy and research.

hour under discussion. One was that a woman friend called him "Herr von Vorsicht" ("Mr. Foresight") because he was so cautious about initiating a sexual relationship with her. Freud then showed the patient the calling card of a Dr. Forsyth from England, who had visited him just a quarter of an hour before. (The patient knew that when foreigners began to come to Freud, with the end of the First World War, he would have to give up his sessions.) What the patient said was: "I'm a Forsyth too: that's what the girl calls me." Freud explains: "It is hard to mistake the mixture of jealous demand and melancholy self-depreciation which finds its expression in this remark. We shall not be going astray if we complete it in some such way as this: 'It's mortifying to me that your thoughts should be so intensely occupied with this new arrival. Do come back to me; after all, I am a Forsyth too—though it's true I'm only a Herr von Vorsicht, as the girl says' " (p. 51).

Freud also suggests a possible connection to the fact that the patient had lent him volumes from Galsworthy's *The Forsyte Saga*, though he does not explicitly link this to the theme of jealousy in terms of its being outside the ordinary run of professional contact.

Freud describes two other associations in the same hour which he suggests allude to the same theme. One was a question about whether a woman named Freud-Ottorego, who was giving a course in English, was a relative of Freud's. But the patient for the first time in the analysis made the error of saying "Freund" instead of "Freud"; a common error in citing his name, according to Freud. The connection between this association and slip and the theme of the patient's jealousy, Freud speculates, is that Freud had shortly before visited a friend named Freund who, it turned out, lived in the same building in which the patient lived.

The third association occurred at the end of the hour when the patient related a dream which he called an *Alptraum* (the German word for nightmare). He then told of his having mistranslated *Alptraum* on a recent occasion. Freud, however, was reminded of an instance when the patient's hour had been interrupted by the arrival of Dr. Ernest Jones, who had written a book on nightmares.

It seems quite clear from Freud's account that he did not, at least in this session, interpret these associations, so there is no evidence to validate this rather complex chain of speculation. Indeed, Freud brings up this vignette in the course of an examination of possible thought transference. Nevertheless, his discussion does raise the question of various real clues which might have been the basis for the patient's associations. We find here a very clear illustration of Freud's concluding that associations not explicitly about the analytic relationship may well allude to it, as Freud indicates in his interpretation of the statement: "I'm a Forsyth too: that's what the girl calls me" (p. 51). One must conclude that while Freud may not have consistently analyzed the transference in the way I have said it should be done, he doubtless often did so.

It is clear then that although the principle of the analysis of the transference was enunciated early, it only gradually came to assume a central role in technique. Laplanche and Pontalis (1967) make the same point in their discussion of the definition of transference. It may indeed be this point that is responsible for the differences in opinion on *when* Freud's technique became his definitive one. If one's definition of "definitive" refers to the discovery of the principle, the date is an early one. If one's definition refers to the thorough integration of the principle into technique, it is later. Kanzer (1966) takes the second view, as I pointed out earlier, in his interpretation of Freud's remarks on the development of his technique in 1920. I have already stated my disagreement with Kanzer's conclusion that Freud did not reach the concept of the transference neurosis until 1914. But I believe Kanzer is right in concluding that Freud still used the transference to overcome resistance. The latter transference is the unobjectionable positive transference. That transference is a necessary ally throughout the analytic process; however, it should be used not to overcome resistance but as the basis of the relationship necessary to analyze the transference resistance.

That Freud on the one hand regarded the analysis of the transference as ancillary to work outside the transference and on the other hand ascribed to it the central role in bringing conviction to the patient about what had been interpreted outside the transference (as I discussed in Chapter 3) indicates well the ambiguity of his position on its importance. It is remarkable how consistently Freud used this two-pronged formulation. As we have seen, in the Dora case he writes that the patient gains conviction about the connections made in the analysis "only after the transference has been resolved" (1905, p. 117). In the Rat Man, he explains: "it was only along the painful road of transference that he was able to reach a conviction that his relation to his father really necessitated the postulation of this unconscious complement" (1909b, p. 209). In the lectures delivered at Clark University in 1909, he stresses that the transference "plays a decisive part in bringing conviction not only to the patient but also to the physician" (1910a, p. 52). Later, in *Beyond the Pleasure Principle* (1920a), he points out that if the patient cannot remember, he "acquires no sense of conviction of the correctness of the construction that has been communciated to him" (p. 18). And again: If the patient can "recognize that what appears to be reality is in fact only a reflection of a forgotten past. . . the patient's sense of conviction is won" (p. 19). Finally, in the "Outline" (1940), he indicates that "a patient never forgets again what he has experienced in the form of transference; it carries a greater force of conviction than anything he can acquire in other ways" (p. 177).

Because his analysis of the transference was in the service of convincing the patient about the past, I believe Freud moved too quickly to the parallel with the past rather than exploring thoroughly the connection between the transference and the actual analytic situation, an exploration which I have described as a generally underemphasized aspect of the resolution of transference. An example of this may be seen in the original record of the Rat Man case (1909b, pp. 251–318) — in Freud's handling ot the Rat Man's fantasy that Freud's mother had died and the patient's remark that his imagined card of condolence became a card of congratulation. While it cannot be emphasized too strongly that one does not know what Freud omitted from his notes, his very next recorded statement is to ask the Rat Man whether it had ever occurred to him that if his own mother died he would be able to marry. The patient responded with the explicit transference remark that Freud was taking revenge on him — presumably for having voiced the fantasy. Freud says nothing about having dealt with this explicit accusation. Even more striking is the fact that — aside from the episode about the woman's genital hair described above (pp. 151–152) — there are no instances in the notes of Freud's making a transference interpretation on the basis of associations not manifestly about the transference. It seems to be always the patient who introduces something explicit about the transference. Even if one accepts the behaviors to which various analysts have taken exception as being in the realm of the personal rather than the technical relationship, one still has to look for their possible repercussions on the transference. The only ones we see referred to are those the patient brings in explicitly, such as his dream about a herring, stimulated by the herring included in the meal Freud gave the Rat Man.

There is little evidence that Freud *systematically* examined the role of the actual situation as a precipitant for transference elaboration, though he doubtless did so in particular instances. In the case of Dora, for example, he describes his smoking as a precipitant for a transference elaboration. He tells us in the case of the Rat Man that the patient saw a girl on the stairs, whom he "on the spot promoted" — making her Freud's daughter, whom Freud wanted him one day to marry (1909b, p. 199). But again, this information is explicitly brought in by the patient. There is no evidence in the case report that Freud actively sought such data.

In his formulation in the *Introductory Lectures*, Freud makes no mention of the actual situation as playing a role in transference. He writes: "We overcome the transference by pointing out to the patient that his feelings do not arise from the present situation and do not apply to the person of the doctor, but they are repeating something that happened to him earlier" (1916–1917, pp. 443–444).

I have also already cited a passage from his recommendations of 1913 which seems to make a sharp conceptual separation between the real relationship and the transference. Again, the implication is that Freud did not search for the real event that served as a point of departure for the transference. Referring to his insistence that the patient lie down, with the analyst behind and out of sight, Freud explains that "its purpose and result are to prevent the transference from mingling with the patient's associations imperceptibly, to isolate the transference and allow it to come forward in due course sharply defined as a resistance" (1913, p. 134).

One could say I am making too much of these passages and that Freud simply failed to mention the role of the present in these remarks. My point is that someone who was systematically persuaded of the role of the present in every transference manifestation would not make such unqualified remarks. The matter is one of emphasis.

On the other hand, several of Freud's comments do indicate an awareness of the role of the actual situation in the transference. First, there is his statement indicating some limits to the degree to which the translation of a neurosis into the transference is possible in an individual instance. Here I refer once more to the passage: "When anything in the complexive material (in the subject-matter of the complex) is suitable for being transferred on to the figure of the doctor, that transference is carried out" (1912a, p. 103). The implication is that there are things that are not suitable for being transferred onto the figure of the doctor because of the reality of the situation. Similarly, in the *Introductory Lectures*, he points out that in the transference neurosis: "All the patient's symptoms have abandoned their original meaning and have taken on a new sense which lies in a relation to the transference; or any such symptoms have persisted as are capable of undergoing such a transformation" (1916–1917, p. 444).

In other places his formulation is that while the actual situation may require some modification of the transference before it can be attached to the analyst, such modifications are sometimes made. In the Dora case, for example, he writes:

Some of these transferences have a content which differs from that of their model in no respect whatever except for the substitution. These then — to keep to the same metaphor — are merely new impressions or reprints. Others are more ingeniously constructed; their content has been subjected to a moderating influence — to *sublimation*, as I call it — and they may even become conscious, by cleverly taking advantage of a real peculiarity in the physician's person or circumstances and attaching themselves to that. These, then, will no longer be new impressions, but revised editions [1905, p. 116].

At the same time the remarks about the unsuitability of some issues for representation in the transference suggest limitations on the ubiquity of the transference and the comprehensiveness of the principle of the primacy of its interpretation. In "Analysis Terminable and Interminable" (1937a), Freud makes explicit the limitations on the transference. In connection with whether it is possible to do something with latent instinctual conflicts, he notes: "The patients cannot themselves bring all their conflicts into the transference; nor is the analyst able to call out all their possible instinctual conflicts from the transference situation" (p. 233). He indicates that the analyst may, for example, make a patient experience jealousy, but stresses that this must come about on its own, without specific technical intent. In other words, the analyst should not deliberately set out "to behave in an unfriendly way to the patient, [for] this would have a damaging effect upon the affectionate attitude—upon the positive transference—which is the strongest motive for the patient's taking a share in the joint work of analysis" (p. 233).[2]

I am not implying that an analysis can be "complete" but only that the significant conflicts can and will appear in the transference. Nor am I in any way disagreeing with Freud's insistence that the transference should not be manipulated.

A variant of the view that there are limitations to how comprehensively the neurosis can become expressed in the transference is Freud's opinion that the course of the transference need not recapitulate the major problems of the neurosis (1912a, p. 104n). Once it is granted that the modes of disguise are many and that the transference can express itself in modifications suitable to the actual situation, it follows that any significant conflict can and will appear in the transference and that there is no inevitable barrier to the analyst's penetrating the disguise.

As I mentioned in my chapter on the principles of transference interpretation, Lipton (1977b) has discussed the disguise of transference by identification, in contrast to the more usually

---

[2] Incidentally, we see in Freud's use of the terms "transference" and "positive transference" in this late article the same distinction between "transference resistance" and "unobjectionable positive transference" that I have stressed throughout.

recognized disguise by displacement. It may well be that closer attention to the manner in which implicit references to the transference may be expressed in disguised forms in material which is not manifestly about the transference will lead to the recognition that all the significant features of the patient's illness find an expression in the transference, and that therefore the centrality of transference interpretation in the analytic process requires even more emphasis than Freud gave it. Even if this should be wrong, it would be well for the analyst's working assumption to be that all the significant features of the illness will find expression in the transference — lest he be deflected from looking for them.

Another indication of certain restrictions Freud placed on the comprehensive nature of the transference is to be found in his discussion of the contrast between the analysis of passivity in men and penis envy in women. Freud (1937a) points to the strong transference resistance in the male, who "refuses to subject himself to a father-substitute, or to feel indebted to him for anything, and consequently...refuses to accept his recovery from the doctor." But he immediately goes on to state quite firmly: "No analogous transference can arise from the female's wish for a penis." He then describes the female's depressive reactions, which arise from "an internal conviction that the analysis will be of no use and that nothing can be done to help her" (p. 252). It is difficult to understand why Freud would not regard this reaction as a *transference*, quite "analogous" to the one he describes for the male. Following Freud's text, we see the male refusing to accept his recovery from the doctor because he will not accept passivity and the female refusing to accept her recovery from the doctor because he hasn't given her what she wants. Without going into the controversy over "penis envy," what I wish to emphasize here is that Freud is placing a limit on the kinds of conflicts that appear in the transference. On the contrary, I would argue that *all* conflicts are expressible in the transference.

Freud continues:

But we also learn from this that it is not important in what form the resistance appears, whether as a transference or not. The decisive thing remains that the resistance prevents any change from taking place—that everything stays as it was. We often have the impression that with the wish for a penis and the masculine protest we have penetrated through all the psychological strata and have reached bedrock, and that thus our activities are at an end. This is probably true, since, for the psychical field, the biological field does in fact play the part of the underlying bedrock. The repudiation of femininity can be nothing else than a biological fact, a part of the great riddle of sex [p. 252].

The importance of this remark is that it suggests how Freud's biological orientation interfered with his analytic work. Here he seems willing to concede defeat by saying that we are no longer on psychological grounds but on biological ones, in relation to which psychoanalysis is helpless. Freud shows a similar attitude in relation to the negative therapeutic reaction. In that case, Freud attributes defeat not to the biological factors involved but to the abstract concept of a repetition compulsion. Again, I do not mean to imply that one is never defeated or that one should never give up. My point is that failure should not necessarily lead one to the conclusion that the problem is not psychological, or that it demands the invocation of a special principle.

In a footnote to his comment above on the "great riddle of sex," Freud adds to his conviction of a biological underpinning (pp. 252n–253n). Observing that men who repudiate passivity to men are often passive to women, he concludes that it is not passivity as such that these men repudiate but "castration anxiety." This remark, like the one about women, suggests that castration anxiety is ultimately biological and to that extent may not yield to analysis of the psychological factors involved. It would seem obvious that there are important psychological and cultural factors which could result in a man's accepting passivity to a woman but not to a man; the recourse to biological explanation thus appears unnecessary.

And yet in the same paper Freud warns against this very biologizing of psychological concepts. He makes the point in saying that he disagrees with Fliess, who "was inclined to regard the antitheses between the sexes as the true cause and primal motive force of repression." Freud claims that, in contrast, he "decline[s] to sexualize repression in this way—that is, to explain it on biological grounds instead of on purely psychological ones" (p. 251).

Fenichel (1938–1939) raises the same question about Freud's view of biology as the bedrock which I have. He writes about Freud's "Analysis Terminable and Interminable":

> The concluding section of his paper holds that we approach with greatest difficulty those resistances which extend into the biological sphere, and by that he means bisexuality. . . . For the man the difficulty comes from clinging to his fear of being feminine. . . . For the woman the difficulty comes from clinging to her *pleasure* in being masculine. . . . This distinction seems highly significant. Perhaps there lies in it an indication that we should be wary of reaching back to biology as long as experiential and social factors can still be operative [pp. 121–122].

To argue for the psychological rather than biological factors in bisexuality is not to belittle the difficulties in overcoming resistances stemming from bisexuality, but it is to say that they can be expressed in the transference and may therefore be amenable to psychological influences, whereas to see them as biological is to foreclose the issue. Clearly, any theoretical bias on the analyst's part will interfere with his attention to how the issue is being expressed in the transference, that is, it will influence his behavior in the analytic situation.

Others have criticized Freud's writings and practice in regard to the transference. Brian Bird (1972) believes Freud retreated from his initial understanding of transference. He comments on how sparse Freud's writings on transference are, considering how central the transference is. He says: "Although the role of transference as the *sine qua non* of analysis was and is widely accepted, and was so stated by Freud from the first, it has almost never been acclaimed for having brought about an entire change in the nature of analysis. The introduction of free association to analysis, a much lesser change, received and still receives much more recognition" (p. 269).

He considers the remarks on transference in the Dora case "among the most important of all Freud's writings, outweighing by far the paper to which they are appended" (p. 272). Yet Bird indicates that Freud quickly lost his conviction. "Nothing he wrote afterwards about transference was at this level, and most of his later references were a retreat from it" (p. 273). Bird also refers to Freud's "vacillations, contradictions, and omissions, his very insight and his apparent obtuseness" with regard to the transference (p. 277). He makes the interesting point that in "Analysis Terminable and Interminable" Freud says that no substitute for hypnosis has been found, and he wonders why Freud doesn't consider the transference an adequate substitute (p. 275).

Kardiner's (1977) account of his analysis with Freud in 1921–1922 has recently appeared. Insofar as the account is accurate, it illustrates how Freud sometimes did and sometimes did not analyze the transference. For instance, Kardiner told Freud a dream he had had in a previous analysis. Freud interpreted the dream in terms of the Oedipus complex, with no reference to the transference. He emphasized the patient's sense of humiliation and belittlement by his father, his murderous wishes toward his father, and his wish to replace the father sexually with his stepmother. That night, Kardiner had a dream about people digging in a trench, whom he asked to stop. Freud did interpret this in terms of the transference, saying that the patient did not want him to go on digging up the past.

Now Kardiner relates that when he asked Freud why he consciously adored his father, Freud replied that he was terrified of him and had to remain submissive and obedient "in order not to arouse the sleeping dragon, the angry father" (p. 58). Kardiner then explains that years later he realized Freud's mistake here: "The man who had invented the concept of transference did not recognize it when it occurred here. He overlooked one thing. *Yes, I was afraid of my father in childhood but the one whom I feared now was Freud himself.* He could make me or break me, which my father no longer could. By this statement, he pushed the entire reaction into the past, thereby making the analysis a historical reconstruction" (p. 58). Kardiner goes on to underline his concealed aggression both toward his father and toward Freud. "I made a silent pact with Freud. 'I will continue to be compliant provided that you will let me enjoy your protection.' If he rejected me, I would lose my chance to enter his magical professional circle. This placid acceptance on my part sealed off an important part of my character from scrutiny" (p. 59).[3]

---

[3] Nevertheless, there is some reason to question Kardiner's recollection years later, for he does quote Freud as having also interpreted that, as with his father, Kardiner feared his previous analyst would withdraw his love and support if he learned of Kardiner's murderous intentions (p. 55).

Earlier I cited a passage from one of the technical papers to show the distinction between facilitating and obstructing transference. I shall cite it again because I believe it also reveals the view that, for Freud, work on the transference is ancillary to and clears the way for work outside the transference:

> Thus the new sources of strength for which the patient is indebted to his analyst are reducible to transference and instruction (through the communications made to him). The patient, however, only makes use of the instruction in so far as he is induced to do so by the transference; and it is for this reason that our first communication should be withheld until a strong transference has been established. . . . In each case we must wait until the disturbance of the transference by the successive emergence of transference-resistances has been removed [1913, pp. 143–144].

The "communication," clearly outside the transference, not the analysis of the transference, is what is primary. The very designation of transference as resistance has the same implication.

It is possible that Freud's failure to give the analysis of the transference the primacy it should have in the analytic process has played a role in analysts' failure to interpret the transference more actively despite the fact that it was he who invented the analysis of the transference and who explicitly stated that all the patient's conflicts must ultimately be worked out in the heat of the transference.

CONCLUSION

The point of this monograph is to argue that the analysis of the transference should play a greater and more central role in analytic technique than I believe it does in prevailing practice. The development of the analysis of the transference took place early in Freud's work, and although his use of it doubtlessly grew in sophistication and centrality, I believe it never became as central as it should be. Freud remained of the view that the analysis of the transference is ancillary to the analysis of the neurosis rather than contending that the analysis of the neurosis should take place essentially by way of the analysis of the transference.

I make the argument for this latter position by a shift in emphasis in the conceptualization of transference. Rather than regard transference as primarily a distortion of the present by the past, I see transference as always an amalgam of past and present. Insofar as the present is represented in the transference, it is based on as plausible a response to the immediate analytic situation as the patient can muster. This view implies a shift to the position that the analyst is perforce a participant-observer (Sullivan's term) rather than merely an observer. It also implies a shift from the view of the reality of the analytic situation as objectively definable by the analyst to a view of the reality of the analytic situation as defined by the progressive elucidation of the manner in which that situation is experienced by the patient.

From this view that the transference is a resultant of the interaction between the patient and the analyst it follows that the transference is ubiquitously present from the beginning of and throughout the analysis. It is often concealed, however, because

177

both the patient and the analyst resist its implications. The most common concealment is by allusion in associations which are not manifestly about the transference. The interpretation of these allusions should be distinguished as interpretation of resistance to the awareness of transference in contrast to the interpretation of resistance to the resolution of transference. The interpretation of resistance to the awareness of transference should begin from whatever the patient is responding to in the analytic setting or interaction. The resistance to the awareness of transference oftens renders this point of departure preconscious, so that the analyst has to unearth it. It is, however, often explicitly referred to in passing and then elaborated by allusion in associations not manifestly about the transference. These passing explicit references are important clues for the analyst in his interpretation of resistance to the awareness of transference.

Such interpretations of resistance to the awareness of transference are the necessary antecedents to the resolution of the transference. They begin at the beginning and continue throughout. The unobjectionable positive transference which Freud argued was the necessary context for cooperation in the analytic work — the therapeutic alliance — is not something that has to be fostered by other means. It is promoted by the very process of the elucidation of the transference.

The resolution of the transference is traditionally considered to come about primarily by way of the recovery of the patient's history, which explains the origin of that aspect of the transference which derives from the past. This view is an integral part of the position that the analysis of the transference is ancillary to the analysis of the neurosis. I argue, on the contrary, that if the analysis of the transference is the analysis of the neurosis, the resolution of the transference must also largely take place in the analysis of the transference. I believe it does so in two major ways. First, the clarification of the contribution of the analytic situation to the transference leads to the recognition that the way the patient has experienced the analytic situation is idiosyncratic. The patient must then perforce recognize his own contribution to this experience, that is, the contribution from the past. Second, barring impeding countertransference, the examination of the transference inevitably involves an interpersonal experience with the analyst which is more beneficent than the transference expe-

rience. This constitutes a "corrective emotional experience," not
sought for as such, but an essential byproduct of the work.

This account amounts to an increased emphasis on work with
the transference in the here-and-now — both in the interpretation
of resistance to the awareness of transference and the interpretation of resistance to the resolution of transference. It deemphasizes interpretations outside the transference, whether current
or past, as well as genetic transference interpretations. It has
been mainly criticized for this deemphasis with the argument
that all forms of interpretation have their proper role in analytic
technique and that an undue emphasis on the transference has
the same unfortunate repercussions on the analytic process as
any biased attempt by the analyst to force the material in a particular direction. My reply is, first, that the analyst must be alert
to the repercussions on the transference of his interpretations of
it, just as he must be to the repercussions of any intervention he
makes. Second, the question of the relative roles of interpretation
in the present and in the past can only be decided by research in
which analyses are conducted with priority in emphasis both in
time and importance to the transference in the here-and-now. It
may even be that appropriate relative emphasis will differ from
patient to patient.

I have become persuaded that what I mean by emphasis on
interpretation of the transference in the here-and-now can be
made fully clear only by detailed clinical material. This monograph puts forth essentially only the theory of such interpretation. The nine annotated audio-recorded sessions presented in
Volume II will, I hope, provide the needed illustration.

I close with the statement that I believe that with the changes
in emphasis in analytic technique I am advocating, analytic
technique should be applicable over a broader range of settings,
whether gauged by frequency of sessions, use of couch or chair,
type of patient, or experience of therapist, than is usually considered possible (see Gill, 1979, 1982).

REFERENCES

Alexander, F. (1925), Review of Ferenczi and Rank, *The Development of Psychoanalysis. International Journal of Psycho-Analysis*, 6:484–497.
_____ (1935), The Problem of Psychoanalytic Technique. *Psychoanalytic Quarterly*, 4:588–611.
_____ , French, T., et al. (1946), *Psychoanalytic Therapy*. New York: Ronald Press.
Arlow, J., & Brenner, C. (1966), Discussion. In: *Psychoanalysis in the Americas*, ed. R. E. Litman. New York: International Universities Press, pp. 133–138.
Beigler, J. S. (1975), A Commentary on Freud's Treatment of the Rat Man. *The Annual of Psychoanalysis*, 3:271–286. New York: International Universities Press.
Bergmann, M., & Hartman, F., Eds. (1976), *The Evolution of Psychoanalytic Technique*. New York: Basic Books.
Bibring, E. (1937), Symposium on the Theory of the Therapeutic Results of Psycho-Analysis. *International Journal of Psycho-Analysis*, 18:170–189.
Bird, B. (1972), Notes on Transference. *Journal of the American Psychoanalytic Association*, 20:267–301.
Blanton, S. (1971), *Diary of My Analysis with Sigmund Freud*. New York: Hawthorne.
Blum, H. P. (1971), On the Conception and the Development of the Transference Neurosis. *Journal of the American Psychoanalytic Association*, 19:41–53.
Bordin, E. (1974), *Research Strategies in Psychotherapy*. New York: Wiley & Sons.
Brenner, C. (1969), Some Comments on Technical Precepts in Psychoanalysis. *Journal of the American Psychoanalytic Association*, 17:333–352.
_____ (1979), Working Alliance, Therapeutic Alliance, and Transference. In: *Psychoanalytic Explorations of Technique*, ed. H. P. Blum. New York: International Universities Press, 1980, pp. 137–157.
Breuer, J., & Freud, S. (1893–1895), Studies on Hysteria. *Standard Edition*, 2. London: Hogarth Press, 1955.
Brockbank, R. (1970), On the Analyst's Silence in Psycho-Analysis. *International Journal of Psycho-Analysis*, 51:457–564.
Brunswick, R. M. (1928), A Supplement to Freud's "History of an Infantile Neurosis." In: *The Wolf-Man*, ed. M. Gardiner. New York: Basic Books, 1971, pp. 263–307.

Calef, V. (1971), On the Current Concept of Transference. *Journal of the American Psychoanalytic Association*, 19:22–25, 89–97.

Curtis, H. C. (1979), The Concept of Therapeutic Alliance: Implications for the "Widening Scope." In: *Psychoanalytic Explorations of Technique*, ed. H. P. Blum. New York: International Universities Press, 1980, pp. 159–192.

Daniels, R. S. (1969), Some Early Manifestations of Transference: Their Implications for the First Phase of Psychoanalysis. *Journal of the American Psychoanalytic Association*, 17:995–1014.

De Forest, I. (1954), *The Leaven of Love: A Development of the Theory and Technique of Sandor Ferenczi.* New York: Harper & Brothers.

Dewald, P. (1976), Transference Regression and Real Experience in the Psychoanalytic Process. *Psychoanalytic Quarterly*, 43:213–230.

Dickes, R. (1975), Technical Considerations of the Therapeutic and Working Alliances. *International Journal of Psychoanalytic Psychotherapy*, 4:1–24.

Doolittle, H. (1956), *Tribute to Freud.* New York: Pantheon.

Fenichel, O. (1935), Concerning the Theory of Psychoanalytic Technique. In: *The Evolution of Psychoanalytic Technique*, ed. M. Bergmann & F. Hartman. New York: Basic Books, 1976, pp. 448–465.

———— (1938–1939), *Problems of Psychoanalytic Technique.* Albany: Psychoanalytic Quarterly Inc., 1941.

Ferenczi, S. (1909), Introjection and Transference. In: *Sex in Psychoanalysis.* New York: Basic Books, 1950, pp. 35–93.

———— (1925), Contraindications to the 'Active Psycho-Analytical Technique.' In: *Further Contributions to the Theory and Technique of Psycho-Analysis.* London: Hogarth Press, 1950, pp. 217–230.

———— & Rank, O. (1923), *The Development of Psychoanalysis*, trans. C. Newton. New York: Dover, 1956.

Freud, A. (1936), *The Ego and the Mechanisms of Defense.* New York: International Universities Press, Rev. Ed., 1966.

———— (1954), The Widening Scope of Indications for Psychoanalysis: Discussion. *The Writings of Anna Freud*, 4:356–376. New York: International Universities Press, 1968.

———— (1968), Acting Out. *The Writings of Anna Freud*, 7:94–109. New York: International Universities Press, 1971.

———— (1969), Difficulties in the Path of Psychoanalysis: A Confrontation of Past with Present Viewpoints. *The Writings of Anna Freud*, 7:124–156. New York: International Universities Press, 1971.

Freud, S. (1900), The Interpretation of Dreams. *Standard Edition*, 4 & 5. London: Hogarth Press, 1953.

———— (1905), Fragment of an Analysis of a Case of Hysteria. *Standard Edition*, 7:7–122. London: Hogarth Press, 1953.

———— (1909a), Analysis of a Phobia in a Five-Year-Old Boy. *Standard Edition*, 10:5–149. London: Hogarth Press, 1955.

———— (1909b), Notes upon a Case of Obsessional Neurosis. *Standard Edition*, 10:155–318. London: Hogarth Press, 1955.

———— (1910a), Five Lectures on Psycho-Analysis. *Standard Edition*, 11:9–55. London: Hogarth Press, 1957.

———— (1910b), The Future Prospects of Psycho-Analytic Therapy. *Standard Edition*, 11:141–151. London: Hogarth Press, 1957.

———— (1910c), 'Wild' Psycho-Analysis. *Standard Edition*, 11:221–227. London: Hogarth Press, 1957.

_____ (1911a), The Handling of Dream-Interpretation in Psycho-Analysis. *Standard Edition*, 12:91–96. London: Hogarth Press, 1958.

_____ (1911b), Psycho-Analytic Notes on an Autobiographical Account of a Case of Paranoia (Dementia Paranoides). *Standard Edition*, 12:9–82. London: Hogarth Press, 1958.

_____ (1912a), The Dynamics of Transference. *Standard Edition*, 12:99–108. London: Hogarth Press, 1958.

_____ (1912b), Recommendations to Physicians Practising Psycho-Analysis. *Standard Edition*, 12:111–120. London: Hogarth Press, 1958.

_____ (1913), On Beginning the Treatment (Further Recommendations on the Technique of Psycho-Analysis I). *Standard Edition*, 12:123–144. London: Hogarth Press, 1958.

_____ (1914), Remembering, Repeating and Working-Through (Further Recommendations on the Technique of Psycho-Analysis II). *Standard Edition*, 12: 147–156. London: Hogarth Press, 1958.

_____ (1915), Observations on Transference-Love (Further Recommendations on the Technique of Psycho-Analysis III). *Standard Edition*, 12:159–171. London: Hogarth Press, 1958.

_____ (1916–1917), Introductory Lectures on Psycho-Analysis. *Standard Edition*, 15 & 16. London: Hogarth Press, 1963.

_____ (1918), From the History of an Infantile Neurosis. *Standard Edition*, 17:7–122. London: Hogarth Press, 1955.

_____ (1919), Lines of Advance in Psycho-Analytic Therapy. *Standard Edition*, 17: 159–168. London: Hogarth Press, 1955.

_____ (1920a), Beyond the Pleasure Principle. *Standard Edition*, 18:7–64. London: Hogarth Press, 1955.

_____ (1920b), The Psychogenesis of a Case of Homosexuality in a Woman. *Standard Edition*, 18:147–172. London: Hogarth Press, 1955.

_____ (1921), Group Psychology and the Analysis of the Ego. *Standard Edition*, 18: 69–143. London: Hogarth Press, 1955.

_____ (1925), An Autobiographical Study. *Standard Edition*, 20:7–74. London: Hogarth Press, 1959.

_____ (1926a), Inhibitions, Symptoms and Anxiety. *Standard Edition*, 20:87–172. London: Hogarth Press, 1959.

_____ (1926b), The Question of Lay Analysis. *Standard Edition*, 20:183–258. London: Hogarth Press, 1959.

_____ (1933), New Introductory Lectures on Psycho-Analysis. *Standard Edition*, 22: 5–182. London: Hogarth Press, 1964.

_____ (1937a), Analysis Terminable and Interminable. *Standard Edition*, 23:216–253. London: Hogarth Press, 1964.

_____ (1937b), Constructions in Analysis. *Standard Edition*, 23:257–269. London: Hogarth Press, 1964.

_____ (1940), An Outline of Psycho-Analysis. *Standard Edition*, 23:144–207. London: Hogarth Press, 1964.

Friedman, L. (1969), The Therapeutic Alliance. *International Journal of Psycho-Analysis*, 50:139–154.

_____ (1978), Trends in Psychoanalytic Theory of Treatment. *Psychoanalytic Quarterly*, 47:524–567.

Gill, M. M. (1979), Psychoanalytic Psychotherapy, 1954–1979. Presented at a symposium in Atlanta, Ga.

_____ (1980–1981), The Analysis of Transference: A Critique of Fenichel's *Prob-*

lems of Psychoanalytic Technique. *International Journal of Psychoanalytic Psychotherapy*, 8:45–56.

_____ (1982), An Interview with Merton Gill. *Psychoanalytic Review* (in press).

_____ & Hoffman, I. Z. (1982), A Method for Studying Resisted Aspects of the Patient's Experience in Psychoanalysis and Psychotherapy. *Journal of the American Psychoanalytic Association* (in press).

_____ & Muslin, H. (1976), Early Interpretation of Transference. *Journal of the American Psychoanalytic Association*, 24:779–794.

Gitelson, M. (1962), The Curative Factors in Psycho-Analysis. *International Journal of Psycho-Analysis*, 43:3–22.

Glover, E. (1931), The Therapeutic Effect of Inexact Interpretation. In: *The Technique of Psycho-Analysis*. New York: International Universities Press, 1955, pp. 353–366.

_____ (1955), *The Technique of Psycho-Analysis*. New York: International Universities Press.

Gray, P. (1973), Psychoanalytic Technique and the Ego's Capacity for Viewing Intrapsychic Activity. *Journal of the American Psychoanalytic Association*, 21:474–494.

Greenacre, P. (1954), Practical Considerations in Relation to Psychoanalytic Therapy. *Journal of the American Psychoanalytic Association*, 2:671–684.

Greenson, R. R. (1965), The Working Alliance and the Transference Neurosis. *Psychoanalytic Quarterly*, 34:155–181.

_____ (1966), Discussion. In: *Psychoanalysis in the Americas*, ed. R. E. Litman. New York: International Universities Press, pp. 131–132.

_____ (1967), *The Technique and Practice of Psychoanalysis*, Vol. I. New York: International Universities Press.

_____ (1971), The "Real" Relationship between the Patient and the Psychoanalyst. In: *The Unconscious Today*, ed. M. Kanzer. New York: International Universities Press, pp. 213–232.

_____ (1974), Transference: Freud or Klein. *International Journal of Psycho-Analysis*, 55:37–51.

_____ & Wexler, M. (1969), The Non-Transference Relationship in the Psychoanalytic Situation. *International Journal of Psycho-Analysis*, 50:27–40.

Harley, M. (1971), The Current Status of Transference Neurosis in Children. *Journal of the American Psychoanalytic Association*, 19:26–42.

Hartmann, H. (1951), Technical Implications of Ego Psychology. *Psychoanalytic Quarterly*, 20:31–43.

Heimann, P. (1950), On Counter-transference. *International Journal of Psycho-Analysis*, 31:81–84.

_____ (1962), The Curative Factors in Psychoanalysis: Contribution to the Discussion. *International Journal of Psycho-Analysis*, 43:228–231.

Hendrick, I. (1939), *Facts and Theories of Psychoanalysis*. New York: Knopf.

Kaiser, H. (1934), Problems of Technique. In: *The Evolution of Psychoanalytic Technique*, ed. M. Bergmann & F. Hartman. New York: Basic Books, 1976, pp. 383–413.

Kanzer, M. (1963), Review of *The Psychoanalytic Situation* by L. Stone. *International Journal of Psycho-Analysis*, 44:108–110.

_____ (1966), The Motor Sphere of the Transference. *Psychoanalytic Quarterly*, 35:522–539.

_____ (1975), The Therapeutic and Working Alliances. *International Journal of Psychoanalytic Psychotherapy*, 4:48–68.

———— (1980), Freud's "Human Influence" on the Rat Man. In: *Freud and His Patients*, ed. M. Kanzer & J. Glenn. New York: Aronson, pp. 232–240.

———— & Blum, H. P. (1967), Classical Psychoanalysis since 1931. In: *Psychoanalytic Techniques: A Handbook for the Practicing Psychoanalyst*, ed. B. B. Wolman. New York: Basic Books, pp. 93–146.

Kardiner, A. (1977), *My Analysis with Freud.* New York: Norton.

Khan, M. M. R. (1973), Mrs. Alix Strachey (Obituary). *International Journal of Psycho-Analysis*, 54:370.

King, P. (1962), The Curative Factors in Psycho-Analysis: Contribution to the Discussion. *International Journal of Psycho-Analysis*, 43:225–227.

Klein, M. (1952), The Origins of Transference. *International Journal of Psycho-Analysis*, 33:433–438.

Kohut, H. (1959), Introspection, Empathy, and Psychoanalysis. *Journal of the American Psychoanalytic Association*, 7:459–483.

———— & Seitz, P. (1963), Concepts and Theories of Psychoanalysis. In: *Concepts of Personality*, ed. J. Wepman & R. Heine. Chicago: Aldine, pp. 113–141.

Kris, E. (1951), Ego Psychology and Interpretation in Psychoanalytic Therapy. *Psychoanalytic Quarterly*, 20:15–30.

———— (1956a), The Recovery of Childhood Memories in Psychoanalysis. *The Psychoanalytic Study of the Child*, 11:54–88. New York: International Universities Press.

———— (1956b), On Some Vicissitudes of Insight in Psycho-Analysis. *International Journal of Psycho-Analysis*, 37:445–455.

Kubie, L. S. (1952), Problems and Techniques of Psychoanalytic Validation and Progress. In: *Psychoanalysis as a Science*, ed. E. Pumpian-Mindlin. Stanford: Stanford University Press, pp. 46–124.

Langs, R. (1976), *The Bipersonal Field.* New York: Aronson.

———— (1978), *Technique in Transition.* New York: Aronson.

Laplanche, J., & Pontalis, J.-B. (1967), *The Language of Psycho-Analysis*, trans. D. Nicholson-Smith. New York: Norton, 1973.

Leach, D., Rep. (1958), Technical Aspects of Transference. *Journal of the American Psychoanalytic Association*, 6:560–566.

Leites, N. (1977), Transference Interpretations Only? *International Journal of Psycho-Analysis*, 58:275–288.

———— (1979), *Interpreting Transference.* New York: Norton.

Levenson, E. (1972), *The Fallacy of Understanding.* New York: Basic Books.

Lichtenberg, J., & Slap, J. (1977), Comments on the General Functioning of the Analyst in the Psychoanalytic Situation. *The Annual of Psychoanalysis*, 5:295–314. New York: International Universities Press.

Lipton, S. D. (1967), Later Developments in Freud's Techniques (1920–1939). In: *Psychoanalytic Techniques: A Handbook for the Practicing Analyst*, ed. B. B. Wolman. New York: Basic Books, pp. 51–92.

———— (1974), A Critical Review of *The Psychoanalytic Process* by P. Dewald. (Unpublished.)

———— (1977a), The Advantages of Freud's Technique as Shown in His Analysis of the Rat Man. *International Journal of Psycho-Analysis*, 58:255–274.

———— (1977b), Clinical Observations on Resistance to the Transference. *International Journal of Psycho-Analysis*, 58:463–472.

Loewald, H. (1960), On the Therapeutic Action of Psycho-Analysis. *International Journal of Psycho-Analysis*, 41:16–33.

———— (1970), Psychoanalytic Theory and the Psychoanalytic Process. *The Psycho-

analytic Study of the Child, 25:45–68. New York: International Universities Press.

―――― (1971), The Transference Neurosis. *Journal of the American Psychoanalytic Association*, 19:54–66.

Loewenstein, R. M. (1951), The Problem of Interpretation. *Psychoanalytic Quarterly*, 20:1–14.

―――― (1969), Developments in the Theory of Transference in the Last Fifty Years. *International Journal of Psycho-Analysis*, 50:583–588.

Macalpine, I. (1950), The Development of the Transference. *Psychoanalytic Quarterly*, 19:501–539.

McLaughlin, J. (1975), The Sleepy Analyst: Some Observations on States of Consciousness in the Analyst at Work. *Journal of the American Psychoanalytic Association*, 23:363–382.

Muslin, H. (1979a), Transference in the Rat Man Case. *Journal of the American Psychoanalytic Association*, 27:561–578.

―――― (1979b), Transference in the Wolf Man Case. Presented to the American Psychoanalytic Association.

―――― & Gill, M. M. (1978), Transference in the Dora Case. *Journal of the American Psychoanalytic Association*, 26:311–328.

Namnum, A. (1976), Activity and Personal Involvement in Psychoanalytic Technique. *Bulletin of the Menninger Clinic*, 40:105–117.

Nunberg, H. (1928), Problems of Therapy. In: *Practice and Theory of Psychoanalysis*, Vol. I. New York: International Universities Press, 1948, pp. 105–164.

Payne, S. (1946), Notes on Developments in the Theory and Practice of Psychoanalytic Technique. *International Journal of Psycho-Analysis*, 27:12–18.

Racker, H. (1968), *Transference and Countertransference*. New York: International Universities Press.

Ramzy, I. (1974), How the Mind of the Psychoanalyst Works: An Essay on Psychoanalytic Inference. *International Journal of Psycho-Analysis*, 55:543–550.

Rangell, L. (1968), The Psychoanalytic Process. *International Journal of Psycho-Analysis*, 49:19–26.

―――― (1969), The Intrapsychic Process and Its Analysis. *International Journal of Psycho-Analysis*, 50:65–78.

Rapaport, D. (1958), A Historical Survey of Psychoanalytic Ego Psychology. *Bulletin of the Philadelphia Association of Psychoanalysis*, 8:105–120. (Reprinted in: *Collected Papers*, ed. M. M. Gill. New York: Basic Books, 1967, pp. 745–757.)

Reich, W. (1933), *Character Analysis,* trans. T. Wolfe. Rangeley, Maine: Orgone Institute Press, 1945.

Riviere, J. (1939), An Intimate Impression. In: *Freud as We Knew Him*, ed. M. Ruitenbeek. Detroit: Wayne State University Press, 1973, pp. 353–356.

Rosenfeld, H. (1972), Critical Appreciation of James Strachey's Paper On 'The Nature of the Therapeutic Action of Psycho-Analysis.' *International Journal of Psycho-Analysis*, 53:455–462.

―――― (1974), A Discussion of the Paper by Ralph Greenson on 'Transference: Freud or Klein,' *International Journal of Psycho-Analysis*, 55:49–51.

Ross, N. (1978), Book Review of *The World of Emotions,* edited by C. Socarides. *Psychotherapy and Social Science Review*, 12(14):11.

Sandler, J. (1976a), Countertransference and Role-Responsiveness. *International Review of Psycho-Analysis*, 3:43–48.

―――― (1976b), Dreams, Unconscious Fantasies, and 'Identity of Perception.' *International Review of Psycho-Analysis*, 3:33–42.

―――― Dare, C., & Holder, A. (1973), *The Patient and the Analyst: The Basis of the Psy-*

choanalytic Process. New York: International Universities Press.

Saussure, R. de (1956), Sigmund Freud. In: *Freud as We Knew Him*, ed. H. M. Ruitenbeek. Detroit: Wayne State University Press, 1973, pp. 357–359.

Schmideberg, M. (1953), A Note on Transference. *International Journal of Psycho-Analysis*, 34:199–201.

Segal, H. (1962), The Curative Factors in Psychoanalysis. *International Journal of Psycho-Analysis*, 43:213–217.

———— (1967), Melanie Klein's Technique. In: *Psychoanalytic Techniques: A Handbook for the Practicing Psychoanalyst*, ed. B. B. Wolman. New York: Basic Books, pp. 168–190.

Shave, D. (1974), *The Therapeutic Listener.* Huntington, N.Y.: Krieger.

Silverberg, W. (1948), The Concept of Transference. *Psychoanalytic Quarterly*, 17:303–321.

Sterba, R. F. (1934), The Fate of the Ego in Analytic Therapy. In: *The Evolution of Psychoanalytic Technique*, ed. M. Bergmann & F. Hartman. New York: Basic Books, 1976, pp. 361–369.

———— (1953), Clinical and Therapeutic Aspects of Character Resistance. *Psychoanalytic Quarterly*, 22:1–20.

Stone, L. (1954), The Widening Scope of Indications for Psychoanalysis. *Journal of the American Psychoanalytic Association*, 2:567–594.

———— (1961), *The Psychoanalytic Situation.* New York: International Universities Press.

———— (1967), The Psychoanalytic Situation and Transference: Post-script to an Earlier Communication. *Journal of the American Psychoanalytic Association*, 15:3–58.

———— (1973), On Resistance to the Psychoanalytic Process. In: *Psychoanalysis and Contemporary Science*, 2:42–73, ed. B. B. Rubinstein. New York: Macmillan.

Strachey, J. (1934), The Nature of the Therapeutic Action of Psycho-Analysis. In: *Psychoanalytic Clinical Interpretation*, ed. L. Paul. New York: Free Press, 1963, pp. 1–41.

Tartakoff, H. (1956), Recent Books on Psychoanalytic Technique. *Journal of the American Psychoanalytic Association*, 4:318–343.

Wachtel, P. (1977), *Psychoanalysis and Behavior Therapy.* New York: Basic Books.

———— (1980), The Relevance of Piaget to the Psychoanalytic Theory of Transference. *The Annual of Psychoanalysis*, 8:59–76. New York: International Universities Press.

Weinshel, E. M. (1971), The Transference Neurosis: A Survey of the Literature. *Journal of the American Psychoanalytic Association*, 19:67–88.

Wisdom, J. O. (1956), Psychoanalytic Technology. In: *Psychoanalytic Clinical Interpretation*, ed. L. Paul. New York: Free Press, 1963, pp. 143–161.

———— (1967), Testing an Interpretation within a Session. In: *Freud: A Collection of Critical Essays*, ed. R. Wollheim. Garden City, N.Y.: Doubleday, 1974, pp. 322–348.

Wortis, J. (1954), *Fragments of an Analysis with Freud.* New York: Simon & Schuster.

Zeligs, M. (1957), Acting In. *Journal of the American Psychoanalytic Association*, 5:685–706.

Zetzel, E. R. (1956), The Concept of Transference. In: *The Capacity for Emotional Growth.* New York: International Universities Press, 1970, pp. 168–181.

———— (1958), The Therapeutic Alliance. In: *The Capacity for Emotional Growth.*

188 REFERENCES

New York: International Universities Press, 1970, pp. 182–196.

_____ (1966), The Analytic Situation. In: *Psychoanalysis in the Americas*, ed. R. E. Litman. New York: International Universities Press, pp. 86–106.

_____ (1966–1969), The Analytic Situation and the Analytic Process. In: *The Capacity for Emotional Growth*. New York: International Universities Press, 1970, pp. 197–205.

INDEX

189

ABOUT THE AUTHOR

MERTON M. GILL, M.D., is a graduate of the University of Chicago and the Topeka Institute for Psychoanalysis. He has been a staff member of the Menninger Clinic and the Austen Riggs Center and has taught at Yale University Medical School and the Downstate Medial Center. Currently Dr. Gill is Professor of Psychiatry at the Abraham Lincoln School of Medicine, University of Illinois, Chicago. He is also on the faculty and a supervising analyst of the Chicago Institute for Psychoanalysis. His numerous publications include *Diagnostic Psychological Testing* (with David Rapaport and Roy Schafer), *Hypnotherapy* and *Hypnosis and Related States* (both with Margaret Brenman), *Topography and Systems in Psychoanalytic Theory,* and *Freud's 'Project' Reassessed* (with Karl Pribram). He is also the editor of *The Collected Papers of David Rapaport* and a co-editor of *Psychology versus Metapsychology* (with Philip S. Holzman).

PSYCHOLOGICAL ISSUES

PSYCHOLOGICAL ISSUES